SPIES AND SPECIAL FORCES

True stories of intrigue, courage, and camouflage

by Jim Eldridge

SCHOLASTIC INC.

New York   Toronto   London   Auckland   Sydney

Mexico City   New Delhi   Hong Kong   Buenos Aires

ISBN 0-439-43119-0

Text © 2002 by Jim Eldridge
Illustrations © 2002 by Paul Fisher-Johnson

12 11 10 9 8 7 6 5   3 4 5 6 7/0

Text design by Dorchester Typesetting Group Ltd.
Printed in the U.S.A.
First Scholastic printing, October 2002

CONTENTS

SPIES AND SPECIAL FORCES

S pies and special forces are "secret warriors," the ones
who work behind enemy lines. These warriors are in
constant danger of discovery, so they need special skills of
camouflage, deception, or impersonation to blend in with
the enemy environment.

These "secret warriors" are right at the front line when it
comes to physical combat — they are guerrilla soldiers,
often fighting against much larger forces.

Spies operate in different ways. Some play the dangerous
game of being double agents — playing one side off
against the other.

They use intelligence, subterfuge, and false information —
while at the same time they are intent on discovering the
enemy's own secrets!

The motives of spies and special forces vary. For some it is
fighting for a cause. Others — mercenaries — fight for
money, while some seem to simply enjoy the thrill of "the
game," the unconventional victory of the maverick.

These stories are based on some of the world's most skillful
spies and special forces. Who is the best? The most
cunning? The most ruthless? The most worthwhile? You
decide!

1 A.D. 61: ROMAN SOLDIERS AND ANCIENT BRITONS: "DEATH ON THE ISLAND"

From 250 B.C. to A.D. 450, a period of 700 years, Rome dominated the known world. At the heart of Rome's domination was its powerful army of professional soldiers who signed on for a period of 25 years.

The Roman Army was divided into *legions*, each legion containing about 5,000 legionaries. The senior officer who led a legion was called a *legatus*. Each legion was split into ten *cohorts*, each one containing roughly 500 soldiers, and these cohorts were led by an officer called a *tribunus militum*. Each cohort was further split into six *centuries*, each century containing about 80 soldiers. The officer in charge of a century was called a *centurion*.

Roman soldiers were taught to fight in different sorts of formations. When they were in battle, the whole army could fight as one mass or could split into smaller groups. Trumpets were blown to instruct the units to change formation. These tactics usually gave the Roman army a strong advantage over their less well organized enemies.

As well as regular soldiers, the Roman army also used auxiliaries, who were soldiers from tribes the Romans had conquered. They came from all over the Roman Empire, from countries such as Gaul and Syria.

The Romans also used spies to infiltrate their enemies and find out their weak points.

THE HARDWARE

Roman soldiers were among the best-trained and -armed in the world at that time. Their weapons included:

Swords were about 2 feet long. They hung from the right of the soldier's belt.

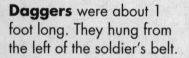

Daggers were about 1 foot long. They hung from the left of the soldier's belt.

Shields were about 4 feet by 2 feet 4 inches and were curved. They were made of wood and leather, with an iron rim at the top and bottom.

Javelins. Roman soldiers carried two metal-tipped javelins into battle. Each javelin was 5 feet long. They were for throwing. They were made of wooden shafts with a section of soft iron in the middle. The iron bent when the spear hit the ground so that the enemy could not throw it back.

Armor for a Roman soldier originally consisted of a vest of fine chain mail. This was later replaced by the *lorica segmentat*, which was a leather tunic with metal strips attached. Beneath this the soldier wore a tunic of wool or linen. Soldiers also wore metal leg protectors called *greaves*. Helmets were also metal.

Footwear for soldiers was a pair of heavy sandals studded with nails.

A.D. 61: ROMAN SOLDIERS AND ANCIENT BRITONS: "DEATH ON THE ISLAND"

The history behind the story

In 54 B.C. Julius Caesar and his Roman army raided southern Britain, withdrawing shortly afterward with just a few hostages. For almost the next hundred years the Romans left Britain alone, concentrating their expansion of empire elsewhere, in places like Gaul (now modern France). Then in A.D. 43 the emperor Claudius invaded Britain, and from that moment Britain came under Roman rule. In A.D. 60 Suetonius Paulinus was sent to Britain from Rome as Governor-General. His mission was to crush the Druids and the Britons and Celtic rebels from Gaul who were hiding out on the island of Anglesey off the northwest coast of Wales. Anglesey had so far proved invincible against the might of Rome.

The governor Suetonius Paulinus was a real person. All the other characters in this story are fictional.

From the journal of Suetonius Paulinus, governor of Britain. (A.D. 61)

    This day I ordered the execution of an auxiliary from the Gaulish cohorts attached to Legion II. Afterward, I had his head nailed to a stake outside my tent as a warning to any others who may be tempted to follow his treasonable example and spread stories that these Druids are invincible magicians. By this act I know I may be accused of practicing the Head Cult which the Druids are known to follow, but if fear of magic drives these barbarian auxiliaries, then I must use the same weapons. We must destroy these Druids and wipe their memory from the face of the earth.

    Our camp is across the water from the Island of Anglesey. On that island are not just the British rebels who have escaped our swords, but also those from Gaul and the other barbarian countries who have fled before our glorious conquest. And ruling over them all are the Druids, those Celtic priests who some of our Gaulish auxiliaries still believe have power over the elements. They are said to be able to raise storms, to make trees walk, to raise the dead. It is said they have witches with them who can make a man's heart burst or stop, with just one whispered word. If I am to win this coming battle, then I need to know my enemy. I need to know all there is to know about these Druids at first hand. I need to know how large the barbarian forces on Anglesey are, where on the island they have their strongholds. To this end I have decided to send a soldier across to Anglesey in the guise of a British slave. I have chosen my man. His name is Castus, a soldier from the First Cohort of the Fifteenth Legion, the son of a Roman soldier and a British mother. He has inherited the looks of a Briton from his mother. He also has the tongue of the British because, according to his cohort commander, Eques Prasutus, when Castus was a child he spent much time in the company of his mother and other women of the Britons. When I heard this, it gave me pause as to his loyalty, but Prasutus tells me that Castus is his father's son, a loyal soldier of Rome and that he has always shown it with unflinching bravery, as befits a soldier of the First Cohort.

Tomorrow Castus is to swim across to Anglesey. He will be posing as a British slave, Ureth, escaped from our camp and running away to join the barbarian resistance. One problem is his appearance. As I have said, he has the looks of a Briton, but as a soldier with the Fifteenth Legion he looks too fit and healthy to have lived as a slave. To disguise this I had him whipped until his back was laid open and then beaten with clubs of wood so that his face and body ran with blood. He took this punishment bravely, knowing it was necessary for victory against the barbarians. When he crosses to Anglesey tomorrow, his wounds will be his provenance and his salvation.

"Is he alive?"

"Who is he?"

The sound of the language brought back childhood memories for him. Thick and rough. British. The smell of grass filtered through his nostrils as he struggled back into consciousness. He could feel the grass wet under him. His whole body ached.

"He's been whipped."

"He is wet. He must have come from the mainland."

"He smells Roman."

"He looks British."

"He may look British but he smells Roman."

Castus opened his eyes. Three men dressed in skins looked down at him, their hair long and matted, the pale sunlight catching on the bronze collars and brooches that adorned their arms and the animal skins they wore. Castus opened his mouth to speak, but his tongue made no sound. He had borne the beating bravely, but the swim across the Strait of Anglesey, even though he had been clinging to a log most of the way, had exhausted him. He had dragged himself as far inland as he could before collapsing. All he needed now was to rest, to regain his strength.

"I say he's Roman. I say we kill him."

No, he must not die now, not before he had even begun his mission! He must get up and fight! He struggled to rise, but then the darkness came over him and engulfed him.

13

When he came round, he was lying facedown on a bed of skins. He was in a small hut lit by torches and a fire. He was aware of soft hands rubbing ointments into his wounds. He began to turn, but a young woman's voice said, "Lie still."

Her hands moved away and then placed more of the warm ointment on his back. He expected it to hurt, but it did not. He sniffed, trying to identify the ointment. A plant of some sort, he was sure.

"Woundwort," the young woman said.

Castus gave a satisfied grunt, and then a bolt of fear shot through him. He had not spoken a word, and yet she had answered his unspoken question as if reading his thoughts. Was this the Druid magic he had heard spoken of by the auxiliaries? Yet he knew that the Druids were men. Was this one of the wise women of whom the Gauls spoke?

The sound of skins rustling as someone came in made the woman stop and look toward the entrance of the hut. Into Castus's line of vision came a man, a warrior.

"How is he?" asked the man.

"He will recover," said the woman. "He is strong."

"Then let him use his strength to rise," said the man. "The council wishes to see him."

The large hut was dimly lit, but torches picked out a bare patch of earth around the central post. Around this brighter circle sat seven men, each regarding Castus intently as he was pushed forward into the light by the warrior who had come to fetch him.

Castus studied these seven men, but kept his gaze lowered. He must remember that he had been a slave, and slaves always kept their heads bowed and their eyes averted.

The garments of five of the men were adorned with golden collars and bronze amulets. The weapons they wore further identified them to Castus as tribal chiefs; he had seen the same costumes and weapons worn by the British chiefs taken or killed by the Romans during their long campaign. Two of the seven, however, were different, dressed in coarse robes with no adornment. The elder of these two had long gray hair with a beard to match, and his gaze seemed to see into Castus's very soul. Castus felt a chill. Was this magic? Did this man know who he was, and why he was here? The girl had read his thoughts, was this man now reading his soul? *O Mars*, he thought, *shield me from this Druid magic! Let me not fail this test.*

The man with the gray hair was the first to speak.

"Who are you?" he asked, and Castus was surprised at the gentleness of his voice. It was low and soothing, a far cry from the shouts and curses of the cohort commanders or the centurions of the legion. He had been told that these Druids were warriors, but what warrior was this, with no weapons, no golden adornments, and a soft voice.

"Answer!" snapped one of the chiefs, and Castus

knew that he would get no sympathy from this man. Suspicion was written large over his scowling face.

"Peace, Yrgath," said the gray-haired Druid gently. "Perhaps he is dumb. He has not been heard to talk yet."

Castus cleared his throat, then he said: "My name is Ureth."

"He claims a British name," commented another of the chiefs.

"Where are you from?" asked the other robed figure, the younger of the two Druids. Again, Castus had the disconcerting feeling that this man, like the elder Druid, was asking the question just to hear Castus's voice, that already he knew the answer.

"I was a slave in the Roman camp across the water," said Castus.

"Why did you come here?"

"I want to be free."

"Who is your father?" This question from one of the chiefs, a huge man with a scar that seemed to split his face in half from forehead to chin. The result of a blow with a long sword, Castus thought. Any man who had withstood that and still claimed kingship was indeed a warrior to be feared.

"I did not know him," answered Castus. "He died before I was born. All I know is that he was of the tribe of the Dobunni and he died fighting the Romans."

"And your mother?"

"She, too, was of the Dobunni. She was taken into slavery by the Romans when I was young. She is also dead."

The chief with the scar nodded.

"So, a Briton," he said.

"I still say he smells Roman," growled Yrgath.

"Of course he does," retorted another chieftan with some annoyance. "All Roman slaves do. It does not make them Roman."

"He could be a spy," growled Yrgath. "Or does Drustan not consider that a possibility?"

Drustan scowled at this questioning and snapped at the warrior who had brought Castus to the council tent: "Turn him around and strip the clothes off his back."

A murmuring was heard from the chiefs as the skin cloak was unwrapped from Castus's body and his wounds were revealed, the whip marks crisscrossing, the blood mixed with the ointment so that his back resembled flayed raw meat.

"Look at his body! Do they look like the marks the Romans would make on their own man?" demanded Drustan.

"They would if they wanted him to pass among us," retorted Yrgath hotly.

Castus knew that, although slaves should be silent, he must answer Yrgath.

"I am no Roman," he said defiantly. "If you kill me for my insolence in speaking when I am not summoned to, so be it. But the Romans killed my mother and my father. The Romans have kept me as a slave these fourteen years. I loathe and despise the Romans."

"Enough," said the quiet voice of the gray-haired man, and the chiefs fell silent at his command. "I suggest we give our new friend the benefit of the doubt, as we have done with all those who seek sanctuary here."

SPIES AND SPECIAL FORCES

To Castus he said, "As long as you are on our side, you have nothing to fear." However, his eyes bored deep into Castus with their unspoken message: "But if you prove yourself false, you will die."

After Castus left the Council tent, he set off on his mission to gather information around the island. His soldier's eyes took in the lay of the land, the cliffs that tumbled down into the sea, the flat areas where a force could land and get fast access into the island. He also watched for lookouts posted around the island and saw few. Just one or two armed Britons watching across the strait toward the mainland, where the Roman army was camped. Although, he told himself, perhaps these Britons did not need lookouts while they had the Druids with their magic powers.

Castus spent the rest of the day familiarizing himself with the island, committing to memory its weak points and the places where its defenses were strongest. Suetonius's orders rang clear in his mind. In the early hours of tomorrow morning while it was still dark, a soldier from the Roman camp would be swimming across the strait and hiding in a wooded cove at the east of the island. Castus was to make contact with the soldier in the morning and draw a map of the island with the British defenses marked. The swimmer would wait until darkness fell again and then swim back to the Roman camp. Castus knew the invasion would follow soon after, before the British defensive positions were changed.

That night, with darkness fallen, Castus joined the Britons around the campfire, but kept to the outer ring, where the orange light from the flame faded to near darkness. He listened to the talk of the Romans across the strait, of the Druids, of magic, listening for anything that he could put in his report that would help the invading force. As he listened he thought: What fools these British are. The might of the Roman army is camped just across the water, and they carouse as if there was no real threat. A legion in such a position would be alert every second, yet these Britons sit around the fire and talk and laugh. No wonder the conquest had been so easy. And the stench that came from the bodies around him. Did these Britons never bathe? By Mars, he had known cleaner animals. And yet his own mother had been a Briton. And his father had loved her, that he had known.

This fact had always puzzled Castus. How could a good Roman soldier have anything in common with a Briton? Castus had been told by his commanders that Britons were not even human, they were a subspecies. That was how they were able to live in this damp land.

Yet Castus remembered how furious his father had become if any of his fellow soldiers had said anything against the Britons.

"They are people, just like us!" his father had shouted angrily at one soldier once, when Castus had been just a child. The soldier had been making a joke about Britons being worse than pigs.

It was a long-ago memory. Castus's father had been dead these many years, and since his death there had been no one in Castus's life to say anything good about the Britons.

As Castus sat looking into the fire he thought of his British mother, someone he hadn't thought of for a long time. She had died when he was very young, and for most of his late childhood and his youth he had just been a boy growing up in a Roman army camp, growing to manhood without women. But now the touch and the voice of the British woman brought back memories of his mother. The way she had laughed. Her touch. And he remembered long-forgotten looks of affection between his father and his mother.

Not all Britons are like animals, he thought to himself.

He thought of the red-haired girl who had tended his wounds. She was gentle. And beautiful. Her long red hair hung down, framing her pale face. He wondered what her name was.

Then he shook himself, angry at his thoughts. It was foolish to start thinking these soft thoughts about a Briton. He was here to find out their weak points, to make sure they were all killed. That was his mission. Yet as he drank and looked into the fire and puzzled over these Britons and their strange ways, he could not get the British woman and her gentleness out of his mind.

From the shadows of the trees, Yrgath and his lieutenant, Urien, watched Castus.

"The council is a fool," snarled Yrgath quietly. "This

Ureth is no Briton. My nose, my eyes, and my ears tell me so."

"What are you going to do?" asked Urien.

Yrgath sighed.

"I can do nothing," he said. "The council has spoken." Then he turned to Urien and his eyes narrowed and a cunning smile spread on his face. "But you are not a member of the council. You can do much."

Urien nodded.

"It shall be done," he said. "Tomorrow I shall take him along the cliffs to place him with our defenses. He says he wishes to defend this island. This will be his chance. I shall take Roff with me. He will be my witness when I say that we saw him stumble and fall. We tried to help him, but he slipped from our grasp and crashed to his death on the rocks below."

Yrgath nodded.

"Do not leave it until too late in the day," he said. "I believe this man is too dangerous to live. Make sure he is dead by noon."

As the sun rose the next morning it found Yrgath already up and sharpening the blades of his knives and sword. He wet the surface of the

21

stone and slid the blade of his dagger across it, backward and forward, backward and forward. Other chiefs may let their servants sharpen their weapons, but Yrgath knew his life depended on his sword and knives. A sword blade that was slightly blunt, a spear just a fraction out of balance, and his life could be forfeit. A warrior's weapons were an extension of his body.

He looked up from his sharpening to see Urien and Roff approaching.

"Welcome, cousins," he called. Then, as they neared, he asked in a low voice, "Do you bring us sad news? Is he dead already?"

Grimly Urien shook his head.

"There is no sign of him," he said. "We have searched the whole camp from hut to hut. He has vanished."

Yrgath scowled.

"I knew it! A man up this early is up to no good!"

"Perhaps it is just because he is a slave," suggested Roff. "Slaves always rise early."

"He is no slave, he is a Roman!" insisted Yrgath. He thought for a moment, then said: "He must be somewhere roaming the island, spying. Send Urdun and Fionn to search for him to the west, you look for him to the east."

"Just we four?" asked Urien. "This island is large."

"We dare not spread the word of what we plan for this Roman," said Yrgath. "If the councilors find out what we have done, we will find ourselves at war with them, and we cannot afford that. You four I trust. I trust no other. The more ears know then the more mouths there will be to spill the deed in bragging."

Urien nodded.

"Trust us, Yrgath," he said. "He will be dead by noon."

Castus wandered through the woods to the west of the island, close to the shore. As he walked he whistled a jaunty tune, a song known to all Roman soldiers. It was the signal to whichever of his comrades was in hiding among the trees. He paused and listened, and then he heard the song being whistled back to him from behind a dense clump of bushes. Castus hurried toward the sound, and from behind the bushes stepped the figure of his old friend Vettius.

"Well met, Vettius," greeted Castus.

"Well met, Castus!" responded Vettius. "You have news?"

Castus nodded. Vettius pulled a piece of parchment from his leather bag and handed it to Castus. Castus took a twig, broke it off to form a ragged point, and then used it to etch into the parchment a rough map of Anglesey, with further marks showing where the Britons' main defenses were, where the main camp was, and where the Druids' sacred groves were. As Castus drew he told Vettius of the tribal council and the suspicions about him spoken by Yrgath.

"I thought my mission had ended before it had begun," he said.

"But they did not kill you? Or keep you in a cage?"

Castus shook his head.

"The Druids rule over the tribal chiefs, and the Druids decided that I really was a British slave."

"Lucky for you these Druids were fooled," said Vettius.

Castus frowned, thoughtfully.

"I am not sure if they were so easily fooled," he said. "The chief of the Druids seemed to look into me. I am sure he knew my real purpose."

"Then why did he let you go free?" asked Vettius.

Castus shook his head.

"I do not know," he said. "There is something strange happening here on this island. The chief Druid has said I am to be given sanctuary, but I feel there are others of the Druids who side with the tribal chiefs and do not believe me."

"Politics," nodded Vettius. "It is the same at the Senate in Rome, so I hear. One senator says one thing, another senator says the opposite to defy him. It is about gaining political power."

"I do not think that is the case here," said Castus. "The chief Druid does not seem to me to be a man who craves power for its own sake. And there is another here — a British wise woman — who also seems different."

Vettius looked at Castus suspiciously.

"You sound as if you are becoming sympathetic to some of these Britons," he said carefully.

Castus glared at him angrily and then spat on the ground.

"If you believe that, you are no friend of mine, Vettius!" he said. "These Britons are our enemies and I would kill every one if I could."

But inside his head he heard a little voice say: except the red-haired wise woman.

Suddenly both men stiffened as they heard voices approaching.

"He could be anywhere," one said, his voice complaining. "How are we expected to find him?"

"We must," said the other. "If Yrgath says this man is a danger, then he is."

Castus peered through the branches of the trees and saw the two men, walking down the track toward the woods where he and Vettius were hiding.

"They are looking for me," he whispered to Vettius. "I must go out and meet them, otherwise they might find you instead."

Vettius nodded.

Castus strode out from behind the bushes and headed for the track, calling out as he did so in a loud voice: "Good morning!"

The two men, Urien and Roff, halted, exchanging looks of surprise at finding their quarry so easily. Then Urien switched on a smile.

"Good morning, Ureth!" he called. "You walk early this day!"

"Aye," said Castus as he joined them. He breathed in deeply. "For someone who has been a slave for so many years, the fresh air of freedom is to be well savored."

"Indeed," said Urien, still smiling, and Castus was reminded of an old phrase: "Beware the smile of the tiger, it bares its fangs to show their sharpness."

"Yesterday you said you wished to fight the Romans," said the other man, Roff.

Castus nodded. "I do," he said.

"Good," said Urien, "because we have come to take you into our service. There is a fort along that coast path that looks out over the strait toward the Roman camp. We have been sent to take you there so that you may join the guard."

So this was how it was to be, thought Castus. His many years of military training told him when death was in the offing. He was to be taken along the coast path and disposed of, thrown over the cliffs into the sea. Without betraying his thoughts he scanned the two men before him. The taller man, Roff, was mostly bulk, but he carried both a sword and a dagger. The other, Urien, was smaller, but he looked the more dangerous. He, too, carried both a long sword and a dagger and also a spear.

Castus forced a smile and nodded.

"I will be proud to serve," he said. "Lead me to this fort that I may keep watch."

"This way," said Urien, and he set off toward the coast path. The taller man, Roff, hung back, so that Castus was forced to be second in the line after Urien.

They walked along the track and then began to climb as the track went upward. As they walked, the cliff edge was a mere footstep away. The earth fell away to rocks and sea far below.

"If I am to aid in defending this fort, am I to have a weapon?" asked Castus.

Urien half turned as he walked and gave a short laugh.

"Certainly," he said genially. "Roff, let him have your sword!"

Castus turned toward the taller man and saw him pulling his sword from his scabbard. Even as he did so, Castus realized why he had been turned to face Roff. *My back!* he thought, and he spun around just in time to see Urien's spear lunge toward him. Urien's smile had gone, now there was just a twisted snarl on the smaller man's face as he thrust his spear at Castus, forcing him nearer to Roff. Roff now had his long sword clear of his scabbard and he brought it swinging down toward Castus.

Praise be for stupidity! thought Castus. *If Roff had swung his sword sideways, I would be dead now.* Castus dodged clear of the sword's downward stroke, ducking down and scooping up a stone as he did so. Before Roff could bring his sword around, Castus threw the stone hard, catching Roff full in the face. Roff cried and stumbled back, and in that instant Castus rushed him, kicking out and catching the tall man full in the body. Roff staggered back, then screamed, his hands clawing frantically at the air as his feet slipped on the wet grass at the cliff edge. Then he disappeared, screaming all the way down to the rocks below.

Castus swung around to face Urien. The small man's eyes glared, full of hatred. Urien jabbed at Castus with his spear and Castus barely scrambled to one side, feeling the point of the spear tearing at his clothing as he did so. Castus turned sharply, hoping to catch Urien off balance, but the small man was too quick for that.

Once again the spear jabbed forward and was then snatched back as Castus lunged for it. The heavy wooden handle of the spear then swung around and smashed across the side of Castus's head, sending him crashing down to the ground. For a second Castus's vision was blurred. Momentarily blinded, he moved more by instinct than knowledge, rolling away from where he believed danger to be, at the same time hoping he was not rolling toward the cliff edge. As his eyes cleared he saw the smaller man thrusting the spear downward, the point aimed straight at Castus's heart. Castus scrambled to one side, just enough for the point of the spear to miss his heart, but not far enough. There was a tearing pain in his upper left arm as the blade of the spear tore into his flesh, sinking in deep. Blood gushed out of the wound as Urien pulled the spear head out. Castus saw the look of triumph on Urien's face as the Briton poised the spear again, ready to strike. Suddenly there was a blur and a scream from Urien, and then Urien and his spear vanished over the edge of the cliff.

Castus shook his head as he sat up, his right hand gripping the torn skin around the wound on his left arm, holding it together. What had happened?

Vettius appeared in his line of vision.

"Two less Britons for the governor to worry about," he said.

Vettius tore a strip of linen from his tunic and began to wrap it around Castus's shoulder.

"You should not have followed us," said Castus. "Your job is to get the information back to the camp. If you had been killed . . ."

"But I wasn't," said Vettius.

He gave the linen a last knot to hold it in place.

"There," he said. "You will live. How do you feel? Can you swim?"

"Swim?" asked Castus, puzzled. "Why should I swim?"

"To come with me from this island," said Vettius. "After this, with two of their warriors dead, they won't believe you are just a runaway slave."

Castus shook his head.

"If I disappear now, the Britons will know I was a spy and will tighten their defenses. I must stay here. I shall go back to the camp and tell the Britons I was attacked and defended myself."

"They will not believe you," said Vettius.

"Perhaps not," said Castus. "But it will buy us time. You must return to the camp now, instead of waiting till darkness."

"Agreed," nodded Vettius. "Where is the safest place for me to swim from in daylight without being seen?"

"I will show you," said Castus. "If you use a bush as cover while swimming, any watcher will just believe you to be flotsam."

As the two comrades walked down the path toward the wooded shore, Vettius said, "You realize the army may not invade in time to save you. And if the Britons suspect you after this, they may torture you to get the truth out of you."

Castus nodded. "As a Roman soldier, I know my life is in the hands of the governor and Mars. I do not complain."

They reached the shore. Across the strait, Castus could see the Roman camp — distant, but just a swim away. He would be safe there. But if he swam to safety, Castus would endanger his mission.

Castus and Vettius shook hands firmly.

"Farewell, friend," said Vettius. "We will meet again."

"If not in this world, then the next," said Castus.

Castus watched as Vettius eased himself into the water, taking a leafy bush with him. It was as Castus had said; from a distance it would just look like a broken bush floating in the sea, just more flotsam. As Vettius struck out for the far shore, Castus turned and headed back toward the British camp.

As before, it was the chief Druid who saved him. When Castus returned to the camp, his shoulder torn and still bleeding, and told of how he had been attacked by Urien and Roff and had been forced to kill them in self-defense, Yrgath had raged and demanded this stranger be put to the sword immediately.

"This is no mere runaway slave!" he had roared. "A man who can kill two of my best warriors! And unarmed!"

It was obvious that there were many who agreed with Yrgath, but the gray-bearded Druid urged caution.

"It is true that this man appears to be very skilled in

the arts of a warrior for a slave, but the fear of death can bring out hidden strengths in a man," he said softly.

This was met with a scornful laugh from Yrgath.

The chief Druid nodded, acknowledging Yrgath's skepticism.

"We Druids will consult our oracles about this man," he said. "If they reveal him to be a spy, he will die."

All eyes now turned to Yrgath to see his response. Yrgath obviously was not happy with this decision, but he knew it was not wise to oppose the Druids and their magic.

"Agreed," he said. "But, for our protection, I say let this man not walk free until the oracles have spoken."

"Agreed," said the Druid.

And so it was that Castus was put into a cage. It was a small square box made of wooden branches, firmly fixed together with leather. There was no room for him to stand inside it. He could only squat and be looked at by the curious Britons and scowled and cursed at by those of Yrgath's tribe, who swore vengeance for the deaths of Urien and Roff.

The day passed. The sun grew higher in the sky and then began to lower toward the horizon. Castus wondered when the Druids would be consulting their oracles. And how? And what sort of oracles were they? He knew little of this Druid magic, save the stories the Gaulish auxiliaries had told. And everyone knew the Gauls were still half-barbarians and not to be believed.

Castus wondered what was happening in the Roman camp on the other side of the strait. Had Vettius made it back safely? Even if he hadn't, Castus knew that even now the Roman army would be making its final preparations for the invasion. Whatever happened to him, whatever these oracles said, once Governor Suetonius and the army arrived, all these Britons would soon be dead.

He was just thinking these thoughts when a soft voice close by him said, "Here. You must be thirsty."

He turned and saw the young woman who had cared for him when he first came ashore. She was holding a leather cup. He took it through the bars of the cage and was about to drink, when he noticed what looked like a scum floating on top of the water.

"They are just herbs," said the young woman. "They will strengthen you and help your wound to heal." When Castus still looked at the cup suspiciously, she took it back from him and sipped at it herself. Then she handed it back to him. "There," she said. "Proof that it is not poison, and that I am not in the pay of Yrgath to kill you."

"I am sorry," Castus apologized. "But I have to be careful. So many here seem to think I am a Roman spy."

The young woman looked intently at Castus, a serious expression on her face.

"I do not think it," she said, and then she added in a quiet undertone: "I know it."

Castus looked at her, shocked.

"What?" he said.

"Sssh!" she said quickly, putting her finger to her lips.

"Why do you think that?" blustered Castus. "Just because I killed two men who tried to kill me?"

"No," said the young woman. "Because I asked the oracle to look into your heart and see the truth that was in you."

Castus hesitated, then he asked nervously: "You have that power?"

"We all have that power," said the young woman. "But few of us use it."

Castus fell silent. His mind was in a whirl. He knew he had to deny it, must deny it, but he also knew deep in his heart that it was no use with this young woman. She knew.

"What is your name?" he asked, at last.

"My name is Aithne," she said.

"Do the Druids share your belief that I am a spy?" he asked, cautiously, trying to make light of it.

"Some knew even before you came," she said. "There is a great argument raging at this moment in the Druid council. Some want you sacrificed as an offering to the gods to defeat the coming invasion."

"And the others?" Castus asked.

"They say that what will happen is ordained and cannot be changed in this life."

Castus was silent, taking this all in. And then, in spite of himself, he blurted out: "You must leave. And soon. Before the Romans come."

Aithne shook her head.

"I have my own path to follow," she said. "Just as you have yours."

Aithne squatted outside the cage, looking at Castus, and to Castus she seemed to have the same power as the chief Druid and to be looking deep into his heart. Suddenly, to Castus's surprise, she slid something out from the sleeve of her robe and slipped it through the bars of the cage toward him.

"Here," she said.

Castus took it and looked at it. To his astonishment he saw that it was a very small knife. He looked at Aithne, a baffled expression on his face.

"It is to save your suffering in what is to come," she said.

"Is it, wise woman?" growled a voice. And Castus and Aithne both looked up to see the figure of Yrgath looming over them.

Behind Yrgath stood more of Yrgath's kinsmen and a younger Druid. This Druid was far different from the gray-haired one. This one had an intense angry glare in his eyes as he looked at both Castus and Aithne.

One of Yrgath's men rammed the end of his long staff between the bars of the cage, striking Castus hard and painfully in the stomach, making him double over with pain. As he struggled to sit up, he saw the Druid's hand reach through the bars and snatch up the small knife from the ground inside the cage.

Aithne was now being held by two of Yrgath's tribes-men.

"Take her away!" Yrgath commanded them. "We shall treat her as we treat all traitors."

"No!" Castus implored them. "She meant no harm."

But Aithne was already being dragged away.

That night Castus sat in his cage and watched the Britons prepare for sleep. The whole night he lay awake. He wondered what Yrgath had done to Aithne. Surely they wouldn't kill her? Yet he knew in his heart that these Britons showed no mercy.

There was still no word from the Druids on what their oracles had told them about him, but Castus knew that if Aithne had been told by these oracles that he was indeed a Roman spy, then the Druids would know the same. Why was it all taking so long?

As dawn broke, Castus still had not slept. His limbs ached from sitting cramped inside his cage, and his wounded shoulder troubled him.

As the sun began to rise, he heard voices approaching his cage. Yrgath and his tribal cronies. And some of the Druids, but not the one with the long gray hair and the gray beard. The young Druid with the angry eyes was also here. Even before Yrgath had spoken, Castus knew the news was bad.

"The oracles have spoken, Roman!" Yrgath spat at Castus through the bars of the wooden cage. "They say you are false. But they also say you have been sent for a purpose. You are to be our sacrifice to ensure victory when the Romans finally attack us." To the warriors beside him, Yrgath snapped out: "Take him from the cage! And bind his arms! Anyone who can kill Urien and Roff single-handed is a dangerous man indeed."

The leather straps that held the door of the cage were untied and the door was opened. Castus felt himself being hauled out onto the grass, and his body cried out in pain as his left arm was wrenched.

He felt himself being half walked, half dragged along,

out of the main body of the camp, toward a wooded grove. He was pulled through the bushes and trees and then into the clearing at the center of the grove. The huge structure before him made him gasp with horror. Now he realized why it had taken so long for the Britons to come for him. They had been busy making this: a wooden man made out of branches and twigs woven together. The body of the figure was hollow, large enough for a man to be put inside. The arms were branches hanging down from the wooden shoulders. The head was made from twigs woven together and garlanded with leaves.

The legs of the wooden man were thick tree trunks. And around the tree trunks were piled straw and wood: a fire waiting to be lit.

Again, Castus heard Yrgath's words of triumph: "You are to be our sacrifice!" His heart began to pound with fear as he realized that he was going to be put inside the hollow body of the wooden man and burnt. He did his best not to show his fear. He was a soldier in the imperial Roman army. He would not let these barbarians have the pleasure of seeing a Roman soldier show fear. He wondered if they would kill him first before they set the fire, but one look at the broad grin on Yrgath's face showed that this would not happen. He was to be burned alive. Now he realized why Aithne had tried to give him the small knife: it was so that he could die before the flames began to burn him. And because of that kindness, she herself would die. Possibly she was already dead.

"Mars protect me and save me," he murmured as he was hauled toward the monstrous structure by the cheering Britons. He felt himself bundled roughly into the cage that was the body of the wooden man.

And then he saw, being dragged into the clearing and toward the wooden man, the figure of Aithne.

"A double sacrifice!" roared Yrgath triumphantly. "The spy and the treacherous wise woman! The gods will repay us well for their deaths!"

"No!" shouted Castus. "She is innocent!"

But Aithne was forced into the hollow inside the wooden man, pressed tight against Castus so that neither of them could move. Then the door was shut and tied into place with leather thongs.

I am going to die, he thought. *But my revenge will be the deaths of these Britons at the hands of my comrades. These barbarians will not cheer so loudly when the Roman army arrives.*

Aloud, he said to Aithne: "I am sorry. You are dying because you tried to help me. If I could give my life to save yours, I would, but they will not listen to me. I hope and pray the gods will allow us to be together in the afterlife and perhaps we can be happy there, away from this life."

He felt Aithne's hands take hold of his.

"Do not feel sorry," she said. "I have no regrets that I tried to help you. As for the future, we have no power over what the gods decree for us. But I will ask them for help."

Castus squeezed her hand, all he could manage in this confined space. He looked out through the wooden bars of his cage. There was no sign of the old gray-haired Druid. He wondered if he had also been taken prisoner by the Britons, the loser in the political power struggle that Vettius had spoken of. Outside there was just the baying mob: Yrgath and his followers, and some others in Druid robes.

He saw two of the Britons arrive with burning sticks from the campfire, and he felt sick. He wondered if they would die quicker if they breathed in the smoke. Would he choke before the flames began to touch his skin? His heart was pounding louder now inside his chest, and he did his best to quiet it. *Have no fear,* he told himself. *It will soon be over. Soon you will be in the other life, meeting again all those old friends who have already passed over.* He just wished they did not have to die like this: trapped by fire. His grip on Aithne's hand tightened, and she responded by squeezing his hand back.

One of the Druids took a flaming stick and approached the pile of straw and kindling at the base of the wooden man. The Druid's face showed an expression of delight.

"We offer this sacrifice . . . !!" he began.

And then he was interrupted by a shout from outside the grove.

"The Romans!" came the cry. "The Romans are here!"

The Druid stopped, and his expression changed from delight to shock and then to anger. He started hurrying toward the wooden man, the flaming wooden torch held high. Just as he was about to hurl the torch onto the straw, he suddenly stiffened and then stumbled and fell face forward. The bolt of a short arrow protruded from the fallen Druid's back.

The Britons gaped in shock at the sight. And then suddenly the grove was filled with Roman soldiers, charging in, hacking away with their short swords. Castus realized that they were the advance party, who had crept up on the Britons unnoticed because of the sacrifice.

As the battle in the clearing raged, Castus noticed that the Druid's fallen torch had set light to a piece of dry straw, and the fire had already spread to the rest of the straw piled around the wooden man's legs. Frantically, Castus and Aithne pushed against each other with all their might, trying to burst open the door of their prison, but the leather ties were too well made.

"Help!" he called. "Help!"

Castus's cries turned into choking coughs as the smoke began to billow and thicken below.

To die this way after all, he thought.

He became aware that Aithne had fallen still, and a feeling of anger welled up inside him and he wanted to explode with anguish and fury. This woman had died for him! Then he heard her voice as she began to chant in a gentle voice, and he realized she was not dead. As the smoke curled around her, she was calling on magic to save them. He couldn't make out the words she said; they were in a tongue that wasn't like the British he knew. It sounded so much older: the language of the ancients.

For a second he was sure the flames flickered as if they were about to die down, but it was hard to tell with all the smoke curling around them. Then, to his amazement, the smoke began to thin out and fall away from them.

Suddenly, he heard a crashing sound and realized that a sword was slashing at the leather ropes on the door. Once, twice, the short sword smashed down through the smoke, then the door fell away and Castus and Aithne tumbled out, hurling themselves over the flickering flames. Every bone in Castus's body ached as he thudded onto the ground, but he felt the relief of being free.

"Saved you again, Castus!" A voice laughed.

Castus looked up. It was Vettius, grinning broadly down at him.

All around them, more Romans were arriving, their sheer weight of numbers overpowering the British warriors as sword clashed against sword.

Vettius looked at the figure of Aithne, lying nearby on the ground.

"Who is this?" he asked.

Castus went to Aithne and gently helped her to her feet.

"She, too, saved my life," he said. "She is my friend."

WHAT HAPPENED NEXT:

The Roman army not only destroyed the British forces on Anglesey, they also destroyed all the oak groves sacred to the Druids. But while they were doing this, another rebellion was rising in the east of England led by the warrior queen, Boudicca. This was also put down by Suetonius's army. From that time, Rome ruled most of Britain for the next 400 years.

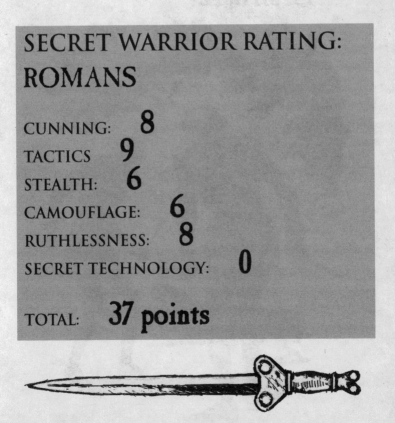

SECRET WARRIOR RATING: ROMANS

CUNNING: 8

TACTICS 9

STEALTH: 6

CAMOUFLAGE: 6

RUTHLESSNESS: 8

SECRET TECHNOLOGY: 0

TOTAL: **37 points**

2 1587: Spies in Elizabethan England: "The Armada Must Be Destroyed!"

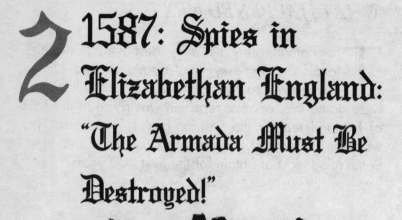

By the Elizabethan Age, suspicion of other nations had become second nature for many politicians of all countries, and spying became official policy under the kings and queens of England. It was developed to its highest level by Sir Francis Walsingham, who became Queen Elizabeth I's secretary of state. Queen Elizabeth spent her whole reign under threat of assassination from many of Europe's Catholic rulers, including members of her own family. Walsingham was determined to protect Queen Elizabeth at all costs, and to that end he set up a network of spies and double agents throughout Europe.

The Hardware

Secret messages were written in **invisible ink**, in those days made from the juice of a lemon; the writing showing only when heated over a flame.

Secret messages, plans, gold, etc., could be hidden about the person, in clothing or in hollowed-out sticks, in belts, or in false bottoms of bags. If the secret article being carried was very small (a precious jewel, for example) it could even be hidden inside a spy's body.

Assassins

Assassins used many different methods, such as **poisons** made from plants. These included **hemlock, foxglove,** and **deadly nightshade**. A concoction would be made from them and added to food or drink.

However, because the taste of these poisonous plants is very bitter, they would have to be added to sweet food or drink to hide the bitter taste. Deadly fungi were also used, including the **death cap** mushroom.

Sometimes assassins used more direct methods, Spanish and Italian assassins preferring a narrow dagger called a **stiletto**.

1587: Spies in Elizabethan England: "The Armada Must Be Destroyed!"

The history behind the story

In 1570 Pope Pius V had issued an order from Rome urging the assassination of Queen Elizabeth I. In 1586 Sir Francis Walsingham, Queen Elizabeth's secretary of state and also the head of her secret service, uncovered a Spanish plot to overthrow the Protestant Elizabeth and place Elizabeth's cousin, the Catholic Mary Queen of Scots, on the throne of England. Part of this plan was an invasion of England by an armada of Spanish ships bringing Spanish soldiers. The English ringleaders of this plot were arrested and executed. The Spanish ambassador to England, Don Bernardino Mendoza, was expelled from England and went to Paris, where his spies in England continued to keep him supplied with information. Queen Mary herself was arrested and, in February 1587, was executed.

Following the execution of Queen Mary, the new pope, Sixtus V, offered a reward of one million ducats to be paid when Elizabeth was overthrown and a Catholic once again ruled

England. It was not long before Walsingham's spies passed him information that a new plot against Elizabeth had been hatched: a Spanish armada was being prepared at Cadiz in Spain to invade England. Walsingham came up with a plan. Sir Francis Drake would take a small fleet of ships and sail right into the harbor at Cadiz and destroy the Spanish ships. To be able to carry out this daring attack meant first spreading misinformation about the destination of Drake's fleet so that the Spanish would be caught off guard. Walsingham's false story was that Drake's fleet was actually heading for Lisbon in Portugal to help reinstate the overthrown Portuguese King Antonio, who was at that time living in exile in London. To spread this false story, Walsingham used his many spies and double agents across the continent of Europe, including top-level officials such as Sir Edward Stafford, the English ambassador to France. But Walsingham's most daring stroke was to send the most famous English playwright and poet of the time, Christopher Marlowe, on a dangerous and deceitful errand.

Although this story is speculative, the events on which it based, and the major players (Christopher Marlowe, Sir Francis Drake, Sir Francis Walsingham, the Duke of Guise, etc.) all existed.

Christopher Marlowe stepped down from the carriage. The journey from England to Paris had been a long one, yet Marlowe did not feel tired, although he knew he must pretend to be. A mission like this excited him, fired him up. He had been followed from the moment he left London. How many of them there were, exactly, he wasn't sure. He had picked out at least three: two obvious cutthroats, one with a scar running down one side of his face and the other with a broken nose. The third was a scrawny little man who pretended to be traveling on his own, but Marlowe had glimpsed the three snatching a brief conversation together when the boat had docked at Calais.

"We expect they will make their move when you reach Paris," Walsingham had told him. "We're fairly sure they will want information from you and so will keep you alive, not kill you."

"You're *fairly* sure?" Marlow had queried. "They will know that I am carrying gold hidden inside my belt. Believe me, Sir Francis, some crooks and brigands may be more interested in getting their hands on that gold than handing me over to their masters for information."

"In this case, if they do, they know their possession of

the gold will be short-lived, because their masters will surely kill them," Walsingham had said confidently.

That's all right for Walsingham, Marlowe thought as he headed along the narrow alleyway toward the doors of the overnight inn. *He isn't here in the back streets of Paris, waiting to be attacked. Accidents can happen. A cudgel that is meant just to disable, or a knife that is intended simply to threaten, suddenly becomes an instrument of murder, however accidental that murder may be.*

The soft tread of a footstep just behind him told him they were making their move. He could hear from their muffled steps that there were two of them. So where was the third? His answer came as the figure of the scrawny little man stepped out in front of him from the shadows of a doorway. *How had he managed to move so fast?* thought Marlowe.

"Pardon, M'sieur . . ." began the little man.

Marlowe didn't hesitate. *Don't make it easy for them,* he told himself. *Make it real.* As he neared the scrawny man, Marlowe gave a sudden vicious kick. The little man gave a scream and fell to the cobbles, doubled over, clutching himself. Marlowe heard the rustle of cloth close behind him, and knew that the two cutthroats had reacted and were even now leaping at him. Marlowe turned and stuck out his right arm, just in time for it to thud into the face of the man with the scar.

The man with the broken nose had stopped, surprised. Marlowe's swift reaction had surprised them. They hadn't expected a playwright to be this fast with his fists. *Well that's because they don't know the sort of man I really am,* thought Marlowe.

The small scrawny man still lay writhing on the ground, moaning. The man with the scar lay in a heap from Marlowe's punch. The man with the broken nose hesitated, and then moved toward Marlowe, crouching low, his huge clawlike hands held out in front of him. *I'd better let him overpower me,* thought Marlowe. He felt annoyed. He'd hoped this would be a good fight, at least. Marlowe moved backward, drawing the broken-nosed man toward him. Three against one and he could have taken them all easily, he thought scornfully. He felt rather than heard a movement behind him, and suddenly a hood had been dropped over his head and he felt the cord being tightened around his neck. *There were four after all!* he thought. And then there was a painful blow on the back of his head and he felt himself falling . . . .

"I asked for him to be brought here in a civilized manner, not dragged here like a bundle of rags!"

The voice spoke in French, but fortunately Marlowe was fluent in the language. The hood obscured his vision, but his hearing was still sound. And his sense of smell. Perfumes. Scents. The touch of fine cloth beneath him on the chair on which he sat. Wherever he had been brought it was no backstreet house. But for the moment he remained slumped and pretended to be still unconscious.

"He would not be brought!" protested a second voice, also in French. "We did not even have time to ask him in a polite way. He suddenly attacked us. We had to defend ourselves."

"Defend yourselves?" said the first speaker scornfully. "Four of you! Thugs! Hardened criminals! And you tell me that this man — an artist, a poet, England's greatest playwright — so frightened you that you were forced to defend yourself. How dare you!"

There were murmurings of apology from the other voices in the room, then the commanding voice snapped out: "Go! My secretary will give you your money."

Marlowe heard the shuffling of feet, then a door closing. Then the voice said: "Loosen the ropes around his wrists. And take that cursed hood off his head. See if he is conscious yet. If he is injured I will have those ruffians hanged!"

"It is all right, Your Grace, I am well, thank you," said Marlowe, moving for the first time as the hood was lifted away from his head.

Claude of Lorraine, Duke of Guise, looked at Marlowe, concern on his face as his servants cut the rope that bound Marlowe's wrists.

"You remember me?" said the duke, surprised. "It has been some years."

"Your Grace is a memorable person," said Marlowe, and he got to his feet to bow, and then stumbled and fell back into the chair.

"Forgive me," he stammered, putting his hand to his head.

"Do not move," said the duke. "Those villains! Believe me, my dear Christopher, I gave no instructions for you to be attacked. I would have sent one of my own servants to contact you and invite you here, but in the current political circumstances it would not have looked good. Certainly not for you."

"Political?" queried Marlowe. "I am afraid I know very little of politics, Your Grace. I am merely a humble messenger running an errand."

"For Sir Francis Walsingham," nodded the duke. "I know." He frowned, and added: "I am surprised to find you part of a conspiracy."

In his turn, Marlowe also gave a frown of puzzlement.

"I know nothing of any conspiracy, Your Grace," he said. "I was asked by Sir Francis to carry out an errand on behalf of the queen. As a playwright whose fortune depends on royal patronage, it would have been foolish to have refused. I have a new play coming out soon, and the attendance by the queen at its opening will guarantee a healthy financial return."

"Of course," nodded the duke. Then he added apologetically: "Forgive me, I am forgetting my manners. You must be hungry and thirsty after your long journey and especially the dreadful experience." He clicked his fingers and a servant appeared. The duke gave orders for a table to be prepared and for the best guest room to be made up.

"I cannot stay," protested Marlowe. "I have an errand to perform. . . ."

"One more night will make no difference," said the duke. "And at this time of night it is difficult to find a carriage to . . . wherever it is you are going."

"South," said Marlowe.

"Ah, south," nodded the duke. "And might one inquire *where* in the south?"

Marlowe smiled.

"In view of what you said about a political conspiracy, would it be wise for me to tell you, Your Grace?" he asked.

The duke did not smile back.

"If I am involved in politics, it is through no fault of my own," he said sadly.

Liar, thought Marlowe. It was well known that the Duke of Guise was the leader of the Catholic faction in France and his luxurious lifestyle was supported by gold from Philip of Spain.

"You may not know this, but the murder of Mary by your Elizabeth wounded me deeply. She was my niece by marriage."

Marlowe looked grave.

"I am sorry to hear that, Your Grace," he said. "Believe me, I meant no disrespect."

"Of course not," acknowledged the duke. "And if you are concerned that I am asking you to betray your country in its feud with Spain . . ."

Marlowe shook his head.

"My errand has nothing to do with Spain, Your Grace," he said.

"No?" queried the duke. His face brightened. "I am glad. My admiration for your work as an artist, and for you as a man, means I would be deeply troubled to ask you to do anything against your conscience." He looked at Marlowe quizzically. "So, if not Spain . . .?"

"I am bound for Lisbon," said Marlowe. "I am sure it

is not an official secret." Then he laughed and added, "although everything that Sir Francis Walsingham does seems to be treated as one."

The duke laughed.

"It is true," he said. "The good Sir Francis has very little humor about him. And the purpose of your visit?"

Marlowe shrugged.

"There is no reason for me to hide it. I am to deliver some money."

"To whom?"

Marlowe shrugged again.

"I do not know. I was told to be in a certain place at a certain time, and I will be approached by someone who will ask for me by name. I am to hand over the gold to them. And that's all there is to it." He leaned forward and added conspiratorially, "I believe it is repayment of a debt, and rumor tells me that the queen herself is making repayment."

"A debt? To whom? For what?"

Marlowe shook his head.

"I do not ask questions," he said. "That way I have more chance of keeping my head on my neck. Our queen has a harsh way with people who displease her."

"True," nodded the duke. "So when those ruffians stopped you . . .?"

"I thought they were robbers," said Marlowe. "I was not going to be the one to return to London to tell Sir Francis I had been robbed of the gold. The queen would have been very displeased with me if that had happened."

The duke nodded again and then sighed apologetically.

"I can only apologize for their appalling behavior, my friend. There are no excuses. Please accept my word that it will not happen again on this journey. I will make sure you are escorted to Lisbon by my own servants."

"I'm not sure if that's a good idea," said Marlowe. "Especially in view of what you said about 'political conspiracy.'"

"You are right," said the duke. "Very well. Then I suggest you rest tonight, and tomorrow we will arrange for a seat on a coach to Lisbon." With a smile, he gestured toward the door. "I hope that my chef and servants have prepared our meal by now." Turning to one of the servants, he said, "Gaspard, will you take Mr. Marlowe to the dining room." To Marlowe he added with an apologetic smile, "I will be with you immediately. There is just one small piece of urgent business I have to conduct first."

Marlowe smiled gratefully and followed the servant out of the room.

The duke waited until he was sure that Marlowe and the servant were well out of sight, and then he strode to a door set into the paneled wall and pulled it open. Into the room stepped a short, thin man with a serious and intense expression on his face.

"Well, Mendoza?" asked the duke.

Bernardino Mendoza, the head of King Philip's secret service, nodded. "So, Lisbon again. It tallies with the information we already have. From very reliable sources."

"Including Sir Edward Stafford," said the duke.

"And from my agent within the exiled court of King Antonio, Antonio de Vega," agreed Mendoza. "The

English obviously plan to invade Lisbon and put Antonio back on the throne. In this way they hope to ruin our alliance with the Portuguese."

"So the reports we had before, that Drake's fleet is headed for either the Azores or the Indies to get more plunder . . ." began the duke.

"Were lies to cover up the true story about the attack on Lisbon!" finished Mendoza. With a chuckle of triumph, he added, "Sir Francis Walsingham thinks he has been clever, but he is not clever enough to pull the wool over Bernardino Mendoza's eyes. I will send messages to our comrades in Portugal so they can prepare."

The duke gestured toward the door.

"And what of Marlowe?" he asked.

Mendoza sneered.

"He is nothing. An errand boy carrying gold for his queen."

The duke bridled.

"I have seen his plays and read his poems. He is one of the greatest artists alive today. It is a pity he is English and not French or Spanish." The Duke then looked intently at Mendoza, and there was no mistaking the threat in his voice as he said, "I would be very upset if anything were to happen to him on his way to Lisbon."

Mendoza hesitated, then shrugged.

"It shall be done," he said. "I will have my agents keep a watchful eye on him." He smiled and added, "It will be useful information for our cause to see the person he hands this gold to."

SPIES AND SPECIAL FORCES

S ir Francis Drake stood on the deck of the *Elizabeth Bonaventura* as the magnificent flagship of the fleet sailed into Cadiz harbor. Behind the *Bonaventura* came the rest of Drake's fleet: *The Golden Lion, Rainbow,* and *Dreadnought,* each at 500 tons almost as large as the *Bonaventura.* With them came the warships *Elizabeth, White Lion, Hawkins, Drake,* and *Thomas,* and the smaller merchant ships, *Susan, Merchant Royal, Edward Bonaventura,* and *Minion.*

Ahead of them, anchored in the harbor or tied up at the wharves, were the warships and other ships that made up the Spanish armada. The Spanish ships outnumbered the English vessels, but with their sails furled the Spanish were at a distinct disadvantage.

Ever since they had left French waters, none of the English ships had shown flags or markings of any kind to show who they were, part of Drake's plan to get in as close as possible to Cadiz without the alarm being raised.

Drake smiled broadly.

"It looks as if Sir Francis Walsingham's ruse worked, John!" he said to Captain John Fenner, the captain of the *Bonaventura.* "Thank the Lord for a cunning and devious mind like Walsingham's!"

"And for a man like Christopher Marlowe to carry out the plan," added Fenner.

Drake nodded.

"Amen to that," he said. "'Tis a pity Marlowe sticks to writing. A man with that sort of courage and daring would make a fine member of my crew."

They were nearing the first Spanish ships now, the ones anchored offshore.

"Time to raise the flag and show them who we are," said Drake.

Fenner nodded and shouted: "Raise the flag!"

The cry was echoed around the ship by one man after another, and then the flag showing the familiar red cross on the white cloth was hoisted up the mast. Beneath it came the flag bearing Drake's own coat of arms.

As the *Bonaventura* flew its colors proudly from its masthead, all along the rest of Drake's fleet flags were raised one by one, announcing to all and sundry that the English fleet had arrived.

The sight of the English flags being raised caused panic and confusion on the nearest Spanish ships. The Spanish had left just a skeleton crew aboard each vessel, a few men to tend each ship before they put to sea.

Drake turned to Belson, the master gunner. "Give the order to fire, Mr. Belson. Tell your gunners to keep their aim above the water line. We want to take as many prize ships back home with us as we can to add to our fleet."

Belson nodded.

"Aye aye, sir," he said.

Belson shouted out, "Give the signal to fire!"

Immediately the flags to relay his order to the rest of the fleet were run up the mast. At the same time the order was relayed to the gunners belowdecks.

On the gundecks of the ships of the English fleet, the gunners set to work. It was dangerous work, but the men manning the guns had learned their trade through years of hard experience.

The chief gunner of each cannon poured gunpowder into the hole at the base of the barrel of the gun. Just the right amount; too much and the cannon might explode, killing all nearby; too little and there wouldn't be enough force to launch the metal cannonball. The cannonball was placed in the mouth of the barrel of the cannon and then pushed down onto the gunpowder by the second gunner, who used a long pole with a wad of wool and leather at one end, called a ramrod. The second gunner then used his ramrod to force a wad of cloth down into the barrel of the cannon to give the necessary resistance for the cannonball.

That done, the chief gunner thrust a smoldering candle into the touchhole at the base of the cannon and set sparks among the gunpowder.

"Back!" would go his command, and all the men of the gun crew would jump back as the gunpowder exploded, hurling the cannonball out of the cannon. The force of the explosion would make the cannon leap as it strained against the chains and ropes that held it in place.

Then more gunpowder would be put in, the next cannonball loaded, and the whole process would start again. And again. And again.

Up on deck, Drake watched as cannonball after cannonball from his gunners blasted into the sides of the Spanish ships, tearing their upper decks and masts apart in a hail of fire and splintered wood. Smoke filled the harbor, drifting across the water. From all the other ships in Drake's fleet, the explosions of cannon fire roared out, and one by one the Spanish ships were being deserted as their crews leaped into the waters of the harbor for safety.

On shore there was frantic activity as the Spanish

tried to get on board their ships and release them from their moorings so they could sail and face the English attack. But there was no time for the Spanish ships to escape from their moorings. Already many of the English ships were close to shore and were pounding the cornered ships with cannon fire. Spanish ship after Spanish ship was being abandoned. Piece by piece, the armada was being destroyed.

Drake smiled in grim satisfaction.

"There'll be no invasion of England this year, lads!" he said.

What happened next:

After Drake's fleet sailed into Cadiz harbor in April 1587, destroying the Spanish ships, the Spanish King Philip, furious at this setback, ordered an even larger fleet to be put together. A year later this fleet, the Spanish Armada, set sail to invade England in 1588. It was destroyed by the English fleet and also by stormy weather.

Sir Francis Drake died in 1596 and was buried at sea in the West Indies. Sir Francis Walsingham died in 1590. Christopher Marlowe was murdered in London in 1593. There were rumors it was because of Marlowe's spying activities. Although today Marlowe's literary legacy has been largely overshadowed by William Shakespeare's, the playwright who followed him and who was partly his contemporary, Marlowe is remembered as a great playwright who wrote, among other plays, the classic "Dr. Faustus."

SECRET WARRIOR RATING:

Christopher Marlowe

CUNNING: **9**

TACTICS: **8**

STEALTH: **6**

CAMOUFLAGE: **2**

RUTHLESSNESS: **4**

SECRET TECHNOLOGY: **0**

TOTAL: **29 points**

3 1863: THE AMERICAN CIVIL WAR: "MOSBY'S CONFEDERACY"

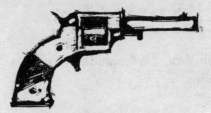

The history of guerrilla fighting is a long and bloody one. The people of a country that has been invaded and conquered by another often resort to secret resistance. This means small groups of people attacking the invaders in surprise ambushes and doing their best to keep their identity secret. Although the United States of America is one nation, during the American Civil War (1861–1865), the South definitely considered itself a separate country from the North and had separated itself from the Union to form the Confederate States of America. The Confederate soldiers sometimes used guerilla tactics to fight off the Union soldiers.

THE HARDWARE

During the American Civil War, the Confederate side used the following weapons:

Rifles:

There was no standard issue of rifles or pistols for the Confederate side during the Civil War. We have highlighted those that were used mainly in Virginia.

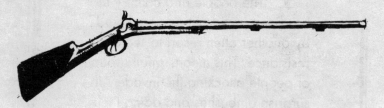

M1855. The M1855 was a Confederate copy produced in Richmond, Virginia, of the M1855 rifle musket used by the Union forces. Muzzle velocity: 950 feet per second. At 1,000 yards it could penetrate 3.25 inches of wood.

"Richmonds." These were rifles captured from the Union side by the Confederacy. Over 300,000 were issued to Confederate troops.

"Enfields." Rifles imported from Britain. These were British-made copies of the British Army's 1853 rifle musket.

Pistols:

As with rifles, there was no standard issue of pistols on the Confederate side. Individual officers tended to choose their own. These included:

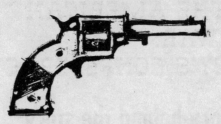

Colt Navy 0.36 caliber pistol. Six-shot percussion revolver.

Colt Army 0.44 caliber pistol. Again, a six-shot percussion revolver, but heavier than the Navy version.

Adams & Deane 0.44 caliber revolver. Imported from Britain.

Swords & sabers:
Most Confederate officers carried a sword or a saber. However, John Singleton Mosby (the subject of our story) declined to use one, saying it was no match for a pistol.

Sword. The regulation sword had a 32-inch-long straight blade with a guard at the hilt.

Saber. The field officers' version of the sword, carried by majors and above, had a slightly curved engraved blade, with an elaborately cast hilt.

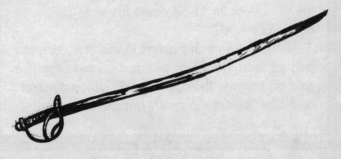

1863: THE AMERICAN CIVIL WAR: "MOSBY'S CONFEDERACY"

The history behind the story

In 1861 the American Civil War between the Northern states (the Union) and the Southern states (the Confederacy) began. On the surface the War was about slavery: the North calling for the abolition of slavery, the South wanting to keep it. However, for many Southerners the war was about more than just slavery, it was about independence from an alien government. One such Southerner was lawyer John Singleton Mosby from Virginia. Captain (later Colonel) Mosby led his small band of partisans, the 43rd Battalion of Virginia Cavalry, in guerrilla raids against the might of the Union army. Mosby's troop was possibly the most successful Confederate guerrilla unit operating during the Civil War. In 1863 came his most audacious raid.

All the leading characters in this story actually existed, and the major events depicted here (the raid on Fairfax, the capture of a Union general and other officers) actually happened.

"Well?" demanded Major General Philip Sheridan.

He could tell it was bad news just from the look on the lieutenant's face.

"One of our supply trains was held up and robbed last night, sir," said the lieutenant unhappily. "They left the food behind, but they took the guns and horses."

"How many guns and horses?" demanded Sheridan.

The lieutenant mumbled a figure in a low voice.

"Speak up!" snapped Sheridan. "How many guns and horses did they take?"

"Five hundred guns, one hundred horses," repeated the lieutenant.

"Let me guess," growled Sheridan. "Did this take place in Virginia?"

The lieutenant nodded.

"Mosby!" snapped Sheridan.

"It looks as if it was him," agreed the lieutenant. "The train driver said the leader of the raiders had a big feather in his hat."

Sheridan slammed his fist down hard onto his desk. Mosby again! The man was a thorn in his side. Over a thousand of his Union soldiers were tied up trawling the roads of Virginia fighting against this one man and his band of farmers.

"Why can't we catch him?" he demanded.

"He's hard to find, sir," said the lieutenant.

"He rides around the countryside wearing a hat with a huge feather in it and a long cape with red silk lining!" raged Sheridan. "How hard is anyone to find, looking like that!"

"He doesn't always dress like that, sir. Only when he and his men are on a raid."

Sheridan shook his head.

"If we can't beat a few Southern farmers led by some backwoods lawyer, I sometimes wonder what hope we have of winning this war," he groaned.

"Shall I send more men after Mosby, sir?" asked the lieutenant.

"We already have a thousand men scouring Virginia for him," fumed Sheridan. Then he nodded. "All right, send more. But make sure they have a professional soldier leading them. Who are our commanding officers nearest to where Mosby's operating?"

"It's hard to say, sir. Mosby seems to operate at will all over east Virginia. But Colonel Wyndham and General Stoughton are quartered at Fairfax with their troops."

Sheridan shook his head again.

"Mosby's been running rings around Wyndham these last few months. Send a message to General Stoughton. Tell him I want Mosby and those partisans of his captured, and I want them brought here to Washington so I can see face-to-face just what sort of man this Mosby is."

"Halt!" came the whispered command from the front of the column, and the twenty-nine men riding behind their leader pulled their mounts to a halt as the word was passed back along the line.

Captain John Singleton Mosby sat astride his horse and scanned the darkness of the two roads ahead and strained his ears for any sounds. None came.

"Looks kinda quiet, sir," whispered Walter Frankland on his left. "Yankees must be somewhere else tonight."

Mosby nodded, but added: "How things look is not necessarily how they are, Walter. And as long as we bear that in mind, with luck we'll keep one step ahead of the Yankees."

He considered their position. The road in front of them forked in two separate directions, one leading to the village of Chantilly, the other going to the village of Centreville. Both were six miles from the town of Fairfax, their final objective. The day before, word had reached him that a thousand Union troops were stationed in Chantilly. His guess was that at least a few hundred of those would now have been moved on to Centreville to keep watch.

"When we get nearer to Fairfax, I'm sure they'll have lookouts on the roads," he mused. "Our objective is Fairfax itself, which is where we'll find Stoughton and Wyndham. I don't want to waste time with just a bunch of trigger-happy soldiers in blue when we have more important prizes to take."

"So which way, Captain?" asked Frankland. "Chantilly or Centreville?"

"Neither," said Mosby. "We'll go through the woods. And slowly. We don't want any horse catching a root and breaking its leg. And no talking. Pass the word back among the men."

The instructions were passed back, and then the column moved off again. They entered the woods and were soon swallowed up in the darkness of the trees.

Tonight, thought Mosby with grim determination, we'll strike a blow against the Yankees that'll show them we can hit them wherever and whenever we want. We'll capture General Stoughton and Colonel Wyndham from their own headquarters. Just pluck them out from the middle of thousands of their own soldiers. He could imagine Sheridan's rage when he heard the news. And not just Sheridan, but Grant himself. Raiding Union posts had been satisfying, but to capture a Union general would boost morale among the Confederacy to new heights. And there was no doubt the Confederacy could do with such a morale booster in view of the recent setbacks it had suffered at the hands of the Union army.

For once, Mosby's hat was without its familiar large feather, and his long cloak with the famous red silk lining was wrapped up in his saddlebag. Instead he wore a cape and a hat captured from a Yankee officer. If they were spotted by a Yankee lookout, he hoped they wouldn't be noticed in this disguise. In the darkness they might even be able to carry off the pretense of being a troop of Union soldiers on patrol. So far this night their journey from Loudon, in Confederate Virginia, had been twenty-five miles. The last six of them had been behind enemy lines.

They continued their journey, slowly and carefully, until at last, ahead through the trees, Mosby became aware of the glimmer of light in the night sky. It was the town of Fairfax, just over a mile away.

Once again, Mosby reined his horse to a halt, and spoke to Walter Frankland.

"Fairfax is just ahead," he said. "Pass the word back. When we go in, we are a troop of Yankees returning from patrol with Confederate prisoners. Remind the men playing Yankees to sit upright on their horses as if they've every right to be there. No skulking, no hiding. Be open and up front. All the rest of the men, shoulders bowed as they ride. Remember, they're supposed to be prisoners."

With the word passed back along the line, Mosby urged his horse forward.

Soon they had left the woods and were heading for the edge of the small town.

Our advantage, thought Mosby as he rode, is that we Virginians know these towns and villages. We know the streets and alleys. We know the woods and fields that surround them. We know the hills and valleys and the small homesteads. We know where to hide. We know every nook and cranny of where the invading Yankees are stationed. This is our home ground.

The ruse seemed to be working. With Mosby sitting proud and tall at the head of his troop, they entered the town and made their way down the main street. Mosby looked neither to left nor right, not condescending to acknowledge the ordinary soldiers who stood on the wooden boardwalks. He was a superior Yankee commanding officer. Not that there were many soldiers around, just a few keeping watch. It was now past midnight. But all the time Mosby's hand was ready to reach for his pistol if he should be challenged.

As the file of riders passed the telegraph office, three of the horsemen left the line and turned into the darkness of the alleyway to one side of the building. The telegraph clerk would be fast asleep, of that Mosby was sure. The job of the three men was for one of them to cut the telegraph wires while the other two kept watch. There would be no warnings sent from Fairfax.

The file of remaining riders now split into two. Half were under the command of Walter Frankland, heading for a house where Mosby knew that Colonel Wyndham lodged. Mosby led the rest of the men up the main street and pulled up outside the court house. According to his information, this was where General Stoughton had his quarters. Mosby dismounted and strode to the door of the court house and banged on it.

After a few moments, the door was opened and a man looked out, wearing a long nightshirt and carrying a candle, his expression angry.

"Who the hell are you?!" he demanded. "Do you know what time it is?"

"Fifth New York Cavalry with an urgent despatch for General Stoughton," said Mosby. "Just show me where the general is and you won't need to be disturbed further."

"I'll be damned if I'll wake the general up at this hour . . ." began the man, and then he stopped, his eyes wide as he found himself looking down the barrel of Mosby's pistol.

"You'll be damned if you don't," said Mosby quietly. "Where is he?"

All the bluster had gone from the man in the night-shirt. Quaking now, he pointed up the stairs.

"He's in the third room along the first landing," he said. "Please, don't kill me."

Mosby turned to the two men just behind him.

"Keep an eye on Mr. Nightshirt," he said. "And don't kill him." To the others he said, "Joe, keep a watch on the horses. Ames, you and Charlie and Adam, come with me."

Mosby and his three men, pistols drawn, mounted the stairs carefully. There were no guards on the landing. Sloppy security, thought Mosby. I bet they never thought we'd dare to come this far.

Mosby reached the third door along the landing and gently tested the handle. It was unlocked. He pushed open the door, and then struck a match and lit an oil lamp he saw on the sideboard.

The man in the bed, General Stoughton, woke up at this and glared angrily at the men who had disturbed his sleep.

"What in tarnation is going on?" he said. "Have we been invaded?"

"You surely have," said Mosby. "I am Captain Mosby. I believe you've been looking for me."

General Stoughton gaped at Mosby and the other three men in disbelief.

"I'll trouble you to get dressed, General," said Mosby. "And consider yourself my prisoner."

"Has the town been taken?" demanded Stoughton. "I didn't hear any shooting."

"Questions and answers later," said Mosby.

General Stoughton stumbled out of bed and pulled on

his trousers and boots. He pulled off his nightshirt and was examining a row of shirts in his closet, when Mosby snapped impatiently, "This isn't a Washington society party we're going to, General. Put on a shirt now or you'll be leaving bare-chested."

Stoughton glared at Mosby, but a few minutes later he was being ushered out into the cold night air of the street.

Walter Frankland was waiting for Mosby.

"Looks like Colonel Wyndham ain't here," he said. "They say he's been called to Washington."

"Too bad," said Mosby. "It would have been a fine prize! A general and a colonel!"

Frankland gave a broad grin.

"Mebbe we got something that'll make up for it a mite," he said. And he indicated a line of mounted men just along the boardwalk. They were all sitting astride their horses, looks of misery on their faces. Mosby realized that the remainder of his men were covering them with their guns.

"One captain, two lieutenants, and twenty-three men, each with a horse. Plus, of course, their weapons." Frankland's grin grew even broader. "They were just about to set off on patrol when we caught them."

Mosby gave a delighted chuckle.

"Well done, Walter," he said. "This is a fine haul indeed. Right, let's get them to the edge of town, using the back lane, and then we'll let them know what we expect of them."

The file of men on horseback, now sixty strong, rode slowly through the back street of the town, and soon they were at the edge, by the woodland. Mosby gave the order for the column to halt.

"OK, time for all you men to change tunics. You Yankees take off your jackets and hats and hand them to my men. Men, hand yours to the enemy."

Mosby waited while the exchange was made, and then he rode his horse down the line, inspecting the troop.

"Good," he said. "You men are prisoners of war. You will be fairly treated as long as you comply with my orders. If you attempt to escape, you will be shot. We will be passing through some of your own Union checkpoints on our way back. As far as they're concerned, we're a troop of Union soldiers, under the command of General Stoughton, escorting a bunch of Confederate prisoners. If any man tries to raise the alarm, he will die, on my orders. Whether he's a general or a private. Is that clear?"

There was silence as Mosby looked along the ranks of the prisoners, and then General Stoughton spoke up, addressing his Union soldiers. "Men, it is a waste of good Union soldiers to die at this moment. I'm sure we'll all be rescued soon enough, or exchanged, and then we can fight again. If you get the chance to escape, it is your duty to take it. But I order you to do nothing to put your comrades at risk."

Mosby smiled.

"A good political speech, General," he said. "Saying everything and at the same time saying nothing. Still, it will do." To the prisoners he said: "Forget what the general said about trying to escape. With a gun pointed at each of you, it just ain't worth it."

With that Mosby gestured, and the column moved off.

"You won't get away with this," muttered Stoughton angrily.

"Looks like we have so far," said Mosby.

As they rode along the road toward Centreville, Mosby couldn't help but smile to himself. What a haul! And all without a shot fired. It was a good night's work.

As they approached the Union lookout that guarded the road into Centreville, Mosby shot a warning look at Stoughton, who was riding behind him.

"Remember what I said, General," he warned. "There's no need for anyone to die needlessly. We're just teaching your Yankee masters a little lesson."

Stoughton didn't reply, just glared angrily back.

As they reached the lookout the Union soldier on guard called out, "Halt! Who goes there?"

Just our luck to come up against the only alert Yankee private in the whole of Virginia, thought Mosby ruefully. Why couldn't he be like those Yankees back in Fairfax and just let us go past. Mosby pulled his horse to a halt, and the rest of the men behind him did the same.

"Party under command of General Stoughton, taking rebel prisoners to Centreville for questioning," said Mosby crisply.

The soldier then spotted General Stoughton, and he snapped to attention and saluted.

"Sorry, General," he said. "Didn't recognize you at first."

Stoughton opened his mouth as if to say something, then he changed his mind and returned the salute.

"Move on," ordered Mosby, and the line began to move forward again.

That was close, thought Mosby. Then a shout behind him made the hairs on the back of his neck stiffen.

"That ain't no Johnny Reb! That's Randy Perkins!"

"Drat!" muttered Mosby. The sharp-eyed soldier had recognized one of the supposed "Confederate prisoners" as one of his own comrades.

The next second, the Yankee soldier had fired a rifle shot into the air and yelled out: "Reb invasion!"

One of the troops leaned forward and struck at the soldier with the butt of his rifle, but it was too late. Already there were the sounds of soldiers hurrying from the camp. One thousand Union soldiers, Mosby remembered grimly. He reached a decision.

"Make for the river, men!" he called. "Bring the prisoners with us. With luck that'll stop them shooting at us!"

Stoughton glared at Mosby.

"I refuse to run from my own men, sir!" he snapped.

"You ain't got no choice in the matter, general," replied Mosby. "You're our insurance. If we leave you behind, we're dead for sure. Giddap!!"

With that he grabbed the reins of the general's horse with one hand and his own reins with the other, and he jabbed his knees into his horse's ribs, stirring it into a gallop.

His men were with him. As were the prisoners, their horses caught up in the stampede and following the rest. Behind them, Mosby could hear shouts as orders were given, and rifles opened up, their sound deafening as they filled the night air with gunshots.

"Don't hit the men, aim for the horses!" yelled a voice behind them.

"Faster!" Mosby urged his horse.

All sixty horses galloped flat out toward the river, just ahead of a hail of gunfire. The element of surprise had given them a start, but Mosby knew the Yankees would even now be saddling up and setting off after them. All that was needed was for the prisoners to haul back on their horses and they would be overtaken and outnumbered. They had to make the river! If they could get across the river, they would be in Confederate territory. To try to cross by the bridge they had come over would be useless. By now all this shooting would have raised every Yankee in the county and there would be a strong guard on the bridge. Their only hope was to swim the river.

Mosby could feel his horse flagging.

"C'mon!" he urged, calling into its ear. "Not far now!"

Beside him, Stoughton's face was grim. Mosby wondered if the general would try to escape by throwing himself off his horse, but with a chance of being trampled, such an attempt could be suicidal, and the general's face showed that he knew it.

Behind them they could hear the sounds of their pursuers getting nearer and nearer. They were losing ground. And then, suddenly, Mosby heard it . . . the sound of water pouring over rocks. The river.

From the sound of it, it was in flood and there was the chance of being washed away, but it was a chance they had to take.

"Over the river for the South, boys!" he called. "We're nearly home!"

In the moonlight the water could be seen rushing in

white plumes. As they reached the bank, some of the horses stopped and shied.

"Force 'em in!" yelled Mosby.

And, to set the example, he urged his horse into the waters of the river, hauling the general's horse along with him. A series of shouts went up along the riverbank among his men, and then all the horses plunged in and were swimming for the far shore.

Mosby released the reins of the general's horse so that he could handle his own more easily, shouting out as he did so, above the sound of the rushing river: "Don't try to turn him around in this torrent, General. He'll turn over and you'll both drown."

The general knew that what Mosby said was true. The only direction to go was forward, to the opposite bank.

Struggling against the current all the way, the horses and men swam, and then at last they were on the far bank. Safe in Confederate territory.

"OK, head for the woods!" yelled Mosby, and the party pushed their horses at a gallop toward the large wood close by the edge of the river. Once in, they were lost from view.

On the other side of the river the Union posse following stopped at the river's edge.

Mosby reined his horse to a halt in the safety of the trees, gesturing for the other men to do the same. Mosby looked back toward the river and at the Union soldiers sitting astride their horses, looking helpless and frustrated.

Mosby reached into his saddlebag and took out his trademark large feather. He stuck it into his hat.

SPIES AND SPECIAL FORCES

Then he took out his red silk-lined cloak and draped it from his shoulders.

With that he turned to the unsmiling and soaking-wet General Stoughton.

"What was it you were saying about not getting away with this?" he laughed. As he moved his horse forward, leading his men and their prisoners, he couldn't resist whistling. Soon, the familiar strains of "Dixie" were heard, echoing through the night sky. Mosby's Confederacy had struck again.

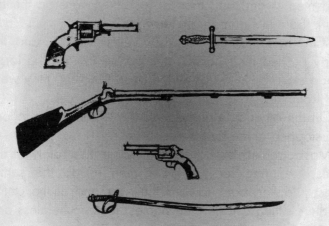

WHAT HAPPENED NEXT:

A few weeks later, General Stoughton was exchanged for senior Confederate prisoners held by the Union side; later, most of the other prisoners captured by Mosby were also exchanged.

The Civil War lasted two more years. In April 1865, after a series of military defeats, General Robert E. Lee, the leader of the Confederate army, surrendered to General Ulysses S. Grant, the leader of the Union forces.

John Singleton Mosby was among many who obeyed Lee's orders and surrendered. Like most of the Confederate prisoners, he was released in 1866. He lived to a ripe old age, dying in 1915.

SECRET WARRIOR RATING:
JOHN SINGLETON MOSBY

CUNNING: 9

TACTICS: 9

STEALTH: 9

CAMOUFLAGE: 9

RUTHLESSNESS: 6

SECRET TECHNOLOGY: 0

TOTAL: 42 **POINTS**

4 1944: Burma, World War II: "Merrill's Marauders"

Following the tradition of guerrilla fighters, who work in small groups against a much larger enemy force, many armies have created their own commando forces. These are sent behind enemy lines, sometimes into the enemy's own country. Their job is to attack the enemy from within by sabotage or destruction — any means that could tie up the enemy's resources. These forces operate deep behind enemy lines, often with the threat of instant execution if discovered.

THE HARDWARE

Assault rifles:
M1 Carbine. Weight:
Empty: 5 lb. 3 oz.; Loaded
with a 30-round box: 5 lb.
12 oz. Length: 35 inches.
Rate of fire: 750 rounds per minute. Size of magazine:
15- or 30-round box.

M1 Garand. Weight: Empty: 9 lb.
10 oz. Length: 43 inches. Rate of fire:
semi-automatic. Size of magazine:
8-round clip.

Pistols:
Colt .45 M1911A1. Weight: 6 lb. 4 oz.
Barrel length: 5 inches. Overall gun length: 9 inches.
Size of magazine: 7 rounds. Muzzle velocity: 830 ft. per
second.

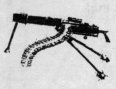 In addition, when fighting behind
enemy lines the Marauders often
found their most effective weapons
were ones that could be used silently,
without alerting the enemy. These
included **knives** and **garrottes**,
which were often chosen individually by the soldiers for
their own particular style rather than using standard-
issue daggers.

 The soldiers were also trained how to
kill using just their **bare hands**.

1944: Burma, World War II: "Merrill's Marauders"

The history behind the story

In 1939 the Second World War began, mainly in Europe and North Africa, between the Allies (Britain and France) and the Axis powers (Germany and Italy). By late 1941 it had become a global conflict, with Japan joining forces with Hitler's Germany, and the U.S.A. entering the war on the side of the Allies. Japan's main area of conflict was the Pacific, and by 1943 the Japanese had occupied many Asian countries. Up until 1943, the war in Burma against the occupying Japanese had been largely fought by British and Indian forces and units from the Chinese army. The Supreme Commander of the South East Asia Campaign (SEAC) was the British Admiral Mountbatten. His Deputy Supreme Commander was the American General Stilwell, whose main responsibility was overseeing the Chinese forces led by Chiang Kai-shek.

In 1943 an American brigade, 5307 Composite Unit (Provisional) began training in India with Orde Wingate's famous Chindits, British guerrilla fighters who had been fighting with great success behind enemy lines in Burma since early 1943.

In January 1944, 5307 Composite Unit arrived in Burma, and General Stilwell gave command of them to his son-in-law, Brigadier Frank Merrill. From that moment they became better known as Merrill's Marauders. In March, Merrill had a heart attack and command of Merrill's Marauders passed to Colonel Hunter, an experienced regular army officer who had trained this new unit. In May 1944, Merrill's Marauders were sent on their most dangerous mission: to capture the heavily guarded Myitkyina airfield, deep in Japanese-held territory.

In this story, the character of Colonel Hunter actually existed, but all the other characters are fictional, although based on real-life Marauders.

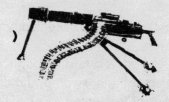

Boom! *BOOM!!!! BOOM!!!!*
The jungle shook as the Japanese planes dropped their bombs, trees bursting into flame, earth and mud and stones flying through the air.

Jake Andrews and Conroy Walton stood up to their waists in the leech-infested waters of the swamp and bowed their heads, protecting their eyes against the flying debris. All around them the rest of the men from Merrill's Marauders, some in the swamp with Andrews and Walton, some on the soft mossy earth, did the same.

More bombs, more explosions, more flying debris and smoke, and then there was the sound of the Japanese planes flying away.

"They nearly got us that time," commented Andrews, doing his best to wipe the mud from his face.

"Huh! They're just guessing, dropping bombs blind," said Walton dismissively. "With these trees there's no way they can see us."

"No, but who knows if some villager hasn't spotted us and passed the word back to the Japanese," said Andrews.

"Are you kidding!" said Walton. "The locals hate them as much as we do. Maybe more, after what they've done to them."

Then Colonel Hunter's voice could be heard bellowing orders:

"Let's move out!" he called. "Remember, we've got an airfield to take."

Andrews squelched forward through the thick, stagnant black waters of the swamp, holding his rifle at chest height, clear of the water.

"Yeh, and only about ten thousand Japanese trying to stop us," he commented sourly.

"You volunteered for this, remember," said Walton, grinning. "You've got no one to blame but yourself."

"Is it all right if I blame the Japanese for starting this war?" Andrews responded archly.

"Who cares who started it," said Walton. "It's our job to finish it."

Merrill's Marauders. Also known as Galahad Force. Official name of the unit: 5307 Composite (Provisional). The only American fighting force in Burma. To the south and west of them, also working their way through the thick stinking jungle, were units of the British force known as the Chindits. Following a couple of days behind them was their backup: 20,000 Chinese soldiers under Chiang Kai-shek. This whole operation had one aim: to drive the Japanese right out of Burma. And crucial to that operation was the part being played by Merrill's Marauders: to take the Japanese-held airfield at Myitkyina and stop the enemy from mounting bombing raids, as well as cut off their supplies. Myitkyina was also a crucial target because it was at the head of the railway line. But first they had to get there, and that meant struggling through jungle so dense, so swamp-ridden, so infested with mosquitoes and every animal that was an enemy of humans, that even reaching Myitkyina seemed an impossibility, let alone fighting a battle against larger Japanese numbers when they finally did. The Marauders had been on this march through this jungle for six days, barely sleeping.

At the head of the column, Colonel Hunter called Captain Carter over.

"I estimate another ten miles and we'll be within sight of Myitkyina. How are the men holding up?" he asked.

Carter shrugged.

"Those with dysentery ain't eating much," he said. "As for the rest, they're exhausted and sore, their boots have rotted in the swamp water, and some have got malaria. On the whole, they're not doing badly."

Colonel Hunter allowed himself a slight smile.

"OK, Carter, I get the message," he said. "Let's find a spot where we can make camp; give them a few hours rest. We need them to be in good shape when we meet the enemy."

They found a suitable spot two miles farther on, where the swampy waters gave way to solid ground. After sentries had been posted, Colonel Hunter let the rest of the men make temporary camp, then feed and rest up before he assembled them for a briefing.

"Right, men, listen up," he told them. "We're not far from Myitkyina. The plan is we get there around dusk and then take cover in the jungle at the edge of the airfield until night falls. We launch our attack at 0100 hours tomorrow morning. By then most of the enemy troops should be asleep, with just a skeleton force keeping the airfield operational. That's what our intelligence says, anyway. If we find they're wrong and the whole place is buzzing with thousands of men, believe me, I'm gonna be the first to tell them."

There was some wry laughter at this from the men, then Hunter continued: "The order of attack is just the way you've been trained. Silent. Like ghosts. We don't want them finding out we're there until it's too late. So keep those pistols in your holsters and your fingers away from your rifle triggers. We're gonna surround one side of the airfield from the way we're coming, the west. There's no fence, just straight onto the airfield. On the signal, you go in in small groups, keeping low, crawling on your bellies through the grass. Locate the guard nearest to you, dispose of him and hide the body, if you can, in the bushes. We want to keep the alarm from being raised as long as possible. If one guard sees another guard is missing, he just thinks he's out of sight or something. He ain't gonna call out an alarm and drop his buddy in it. He finds a dead body, that's another matter.

"Our intelligence reports also say there are machine gun posts dug into the perimeter of the airfield. We don't know how many men at each post. Could be two, could be three. Could be just one lonely Joe on his own. Whatever, close them down, but silently. No hand grenades.

"Captain Carter will be allocating your targets. Some of you will be targeting the barracks, others the airfield control rooms and the stores. Your job is to lock the doors from the outside. Use chains, locks, bars, whatever you've got. The men who are inside need to be kept inside. The more we can keep locked up, the fewer there'll be to deal with. Let's keep our odds up here, guys.

"One more thing. If shooting should break out, don't

show yourself unless you have to. We stay invisible as long as we can. OK, guys, that's it. Pep talk over. Now, better get some rest. We've got a long night ahead of us."

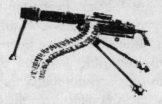

Some six hours later, after a grueling march through ten miles more of almost impenetrable jungle, Andrews and Walton found themselves lying in the long grass that bordered the Japanese-held airfield, along with two other Marauders: Peter Kawalski and Tod Jensen. The rest of the unit was spread out in small groups under cover in the jungle, around the perimeter of the airfield.

The night was dark, like most of the nights in the tropics. The landing lights on the runways were off, but the few lights from the buildings on the airfield gave an eerie glow to the night, just enough to see by. From this distance they could see the guards patrolling, rifles slung over their shoulders. Andrews also spotted a machine gun bunker not far away from them, dug into the ground, the barrel of the machine gun poking out but only dimly seen in the half-light. Andrews nudged Walton and pointed at the machine gun post. Walton nodded and passed the information silently on to Kawalski and Jensen.

"We have to give that bunker a wide berth," whispered Andrews. "Come in on them from the back."

Again, Walton nodded.

Andrews checked his watch. 0055 hours. Five minutes to go. Four minutes. Three. The tension of waiting was starting to get to him. Every muscle in his body seemed to be jumping. Every one of his senses seemed to be more alert than they'd ever been: he could hear the tiniest insect, see right into the dim light of the machine gun post, picking out the barrel of the machine gun clearly. The smells coming from the airfield filled his nostrils: the smell of diesel and oil drifting on the night sky.

One minute. Fifty seconds. Thirty. Twenty. Ten. Nine. Eight . . .

It was time to go.

All around the perimeter of the airfield the men crept out of the jungle, crawling on their bellies, working their way on their elbows and knees though the grass without making a sound.

Andrews was aware of a Japanese guard standing silhouetted barely fifty yards away. As Andrews watched, the dim shape of a figure rose from the ground behind the Japanese guard, and then suddenly both vanished, collapsing to the ground and disappearing as if they'd never been there. One guard down. One large hole opened in the airfield defenses.

Andrews gestured for Kawalski and Jensen to continue on into the airfield and indicated for Walton to come with him as he slid silently across the dew-wet grass toward the rear of the machine gun post. As the two men worked their way inch by inch over the ground,

Andrews pulled his knife from its sheath and held it ready.

They were both nearly at the machine gun post now. From this direction Andrews could see though the entrance into the bunker. Inside the bunker there was just one man on his own, his attention centered fully on the darkness of the jungle outside the airfield.

Andrews motioned for Walton to stay where he was as backup and then edged forward, nearer and nearer the bunker. Then he was at the entrance of the bunker, the knife poised in his hand. The Japanese soldier must have suddenly sensed that there was someone behind him, because he started to turn toward Andrews, but before he could, Andrews had moved swiftly, hurling himself into the bunker, one hand grabbing the man by the hair and pulling his head back, the other flashing down with the knife. The Japanese sagged and Andrews let him drop to the ground. Then Andrews disabled the machine gun. Just in case things went wrong and they had to retreat back into the jungle, this would be one less Japanese machine gun firing at them.

That done, Andrews propped the Japanese soldier back against the gun. To anyone looking casually into the bunker, the soldier was still at his post.

Andrews rejoined Walton, who was still waiting outside the machine gun bunker, and then the two men set off, crawling deeper into the airfield. The grass was shorter now, offering less cover. Ahead of them they could see the dim shapes of Kawalski and Jensen heading for the nearest buildings. Other Marauders were also there, vague outlines rather than definable shapes. So far not one shot had been fired.

SPIES AND SPECIAL FORCES

During the next twenty minutes the Marauders worked their way further and further into the airfield, yard by yard, flitting from shadow to shadow like spirits. One by one, Japanese soldiers were caught and disposed of. As they arrived at each building, every outer door they came to was chained securely.

"This is gonna be a piece of cake," whispered Walton with a grin. "Like taking candy from a baby."

Walton and Andrews approached a small building. A light glowed from inside.

"Lock all buildings," murmured Walton. "Keep them all locked up." He pulled a piece of chain from inside his tunic and was just about to wrap it around the door handle and secure it, when the door was pushed sharply open and a Japanese soldier stepped out.

As the soldier opened his mouth to shout, Walton swung the chain hard and it hit the Japanese across the face, wrapping itself around his head. Walton gave him no time to recover. He pulled out his knife and leaped upon him. Both men fell to the ground, just in time for Walton, because a second Japanese soldier had appeared in the doorway and fired at him. The bullets lit up the darkness as they exploded in a line of tracer just over Walton's head. Then there was the sound of a machine gun, as Andrews opened fire and cut the second Japanese soldier down.

Andrews and Walton stood there panting and then hurried toward the shadows of the nearest larger building, just twenty yards away.

"You were saying?" Andrews cracked sarcastically.

The gunfire had started a chain reaction. All around the airfield were the sounds of shouting in Japanese.

Some of the shouts were muffled and accompanied by the sounds of banging as many Japanese found themselves locked into their barracks or control rooms and tried to batter their way out. Other shouts were clear as Japanese soldiers stumbled out into the darkness.

"Guess there's no need for silence anymore," said Walton, and he opened up with his machine gun at a group of Japanese soldiers who had poured out from a building nearby, mowing them down.

Now the battle turned into a firefight, with the Marauders still keeping to the shadows, using the darkness as they had been trained to do, letting fly with a burst of gunfire before moving swiftly to another spot. The sounds of hand grenades exploding and the dazzling glare of tracer filled the night as the Marauders pressed home their advantage. It was obvious that the swiftness of the attack had taken the Japanese by surprise, especially the fact that the Marauders had penetrated so deeply into the airfield before they had been accidentally discovered.

Within another hour the battle was over. In the dim light it could be seen that many Japanese and some of the Marauders lay dead, their bodies strewn around the airfield. Most of the Japanese soldiers had been caught inside their barracks by the chains locking them in and were now obeying the order to throw their weapons out of the windows onto the ground. If any refused or started firing, a hand grenade was thrown in though the window.

As dawn rose over the airfield, Colonel Hunter stood and watched the Japanese prisoners, their hands on their heads, being marched under armed guard to a secure building. All around, his Marauders were at work, collecting the dead for burial and searching the buildings. The wounded were already being attended to in the airfield hospital.

Hunter looked up to the observation window at the top of the control tower. Captain Carter was up there, preparing the airfield for an Allied landing. Around the edge of the airfield more Marauders were securing the perimeter. Hunter signaled his radio operator to come over to him.

"OK, son," he said. "Send the message to base. Mission accomplished."

What happened next:

The War in Burma continued until 1945. In May 1945 the capital, Rangoon, was finally taken by Allied forces, and the war in Burma was effectively over. Guerrilla warfare behind enemy lines had shown that the might of the Imperial Japanese army could be beaten.

SECRET WARRIOR RATING:
MERRILL'S MARAUDERS

CUNNING: **8**

TACTICS: **9**

STEALTH: **9**

CAMOUFLAGE: **8**

RUTHLESSNESS: **9**

SECRET TECHNOLOGY: **6**

TOTAL: **49 points**

5 1963: The Cold War: "Escape from the East"

The CIA (Central Intelligence Agency) was created in 1947. It developed from the OSS (Office of Strategic Service), which had been the main U.S. intelligence-gathering organization during World War 2. The role of the CIA is to protect the interest of the United States. It does this by gathering intelligence about possible enemy actions against the United States and acting on that intelligence, often covertly.

THE HARDWARE

In the early 1960s the hardware hadn't developed to the level it has at the start of the 21st century (satellites had only recently been launched into space at this time). Nevertheless, the CIA's technology was state-of-the-art, for its time.

Surveillance:
Eavesdropping devices were planted at places used by potential security risks or in enemy embassies. These included listening bugs hidden in walls, ceilings, light fixtures, telephones, pens, furniture, and room accessories.

Espionage:
Espionage usually consisted of obtaining vital top secret information from the other side and was done either by double agents or field agents who gained covert access to sensitive documents. In the 1960s the favored methods of copying top secret documents were:

The Minox camera. The negative could be hidden in a very small object.

The Diebold copier. This resembled an ordinary notebook. A document slipped into it was automatically photocopied.

Microdots. Documents photographed by the above methods could be reduced to a very small dot, the same size as the dot above the "i" in the word "microdot." A whole page of text could be fitted into one dot.

Passing on secret documents:
The dead-letter drop. The best "dead-letter drops" are those that the agent passing on the information visits as a matter of course (a bus station, a library, a regular country walk, etc.). The contact then retrieves the information later.

The brush contact. So called because the agent and the contact will appear to accidentally brush against one another and in so doing pass on documents, sometimes through an exchange of identical bags.

Gizmos:
There were also other unusual devices used by the CIA to gain information. These included:

A chemically treated handkerchief. After one minute of exposure to the open air, it would pick up traces of factory fumes that could later be analyzed to find out what was *really* going on in that factory.

Desk sponges (the type used for wetting postage stamps). These would pick up very accurate traces of body chemistry and would show who (or what kind of person) had actually been in a room during a certain time.

1963: The Cold War: "Escape from the East"

The history behind the story

Immediately after World War II, Germany was split into two administrative areas: the East under the military control of the Soviets, and the West under the military control of the Americans, the British, and the French. Berlin (which was in Soviet-administered East Germany) was similarly split into four zones. At first this system worked well, with all four nations cooperating to rebuild Berlin. However, suspicions between the two major powers got worse. In 1949 Germany officially split into two countries: West Germany and East Germany.

Relations between Soviet Russia and the United States continued to deteriorate, and both countries spent fortunes spying on each other. Berlin was the place where many people tried to escape from the repressive regime of the East into the West. By 1961, over one million refugees had fled from East Germany. So, in August 1961, the Soviet-backed East German authorities erected the Berlin Wall to divide the city. Anyone attempting to get across the Wall and escape to the West was shot by the East German border guards.

In this story, the events and characters are fictional, but based on similar situations of the time.

Berlin. Otto Marck stepped out of the taxi that had brought him from the airport and looked around him. Although, for the moment, he wasn't Otto Marck, he was Otto Klaus. That's what it said on his very professionally forged passport, and he would continue to be Otto Klaus until he got back to the States.

Otto supposed he ought to consider Berlin as his second home town, after Pittsburgh. Berlin was where his grandparents had come from when they came to America in the 1920s. Grampy Josef and Grandmom Katt Marck. They'd left Germany after the First World War to make a new life for themselves and their sons, Walter and Manfred, in Pennsylvania, a place where many other Germans had settled before them. That was where Otto had been born in 1939, the year war broke out in Europe.

Otto had been too young to take part in the war, but, as a CIA agent, he was now taking part in the cold war that followed. The secret war against the Soviets.

Otto went into the hotel and registered as Otto Klaus, a plastics merchant from New York in West Berlin on business, and then went to his room.

"Assume you're being watched the whole time," his controller, Smith, had told him. "Everything you say, everything you do, will be noted by someone and reported back to the Stasi, the East German secret police. The Stasi have their people all over West Berlin. The only safe way is to treat everyone as if they're working for the enemy: every hotel maid, every waiter, every taxi driver, every shop assistant. Assume your hotel room is bugged and your phone is tapped. Trust no one, except our people. And even then, don't say anything to them other than what you're authorized. Remember, if we've got our spies in their embassies, they sure must have theirs in ours."

Otto took off his shoes, lay on the hotel bed, and flicked through the tourist guidebook of Berlin. Not that Otto needed to — he had memorized the street map of the area where he was headed: the Mitte District in East Berlin. This act was for any hidden cameras that might be watching him; he was just another American businessman trying to find his way about the city.

As he flicked through the guide, his mind went back to the meeting with his controller in Virginia just two days before.

"We've got a big problem, Otto," Smith said. "For the past eighteen months, we've been running a top Russian colonel right in the heart of the KGB in Moscow. Prime stuff. What they know about our operations. What the Chinese are up to. Their military foreign policy. Weapons research. Believe me, it's been like getting gold dust."

Otto smiled.

"But now he wants more money?" he asked cynically. He knew how expensive some of these top-level foreign spies could be.

Smith shook his head.

"This guy hasn't been doing it for the money," he said. "In our books, he's one of the good guys. His name's Colonel Varentsov."

Otto nodded in recognition, impressed.

"War hero during World War II."

"War hero plus," agreed Smith. "Wounded in action five times at least. More medals for bravery than most soldiers could hope to get in two lifetimes. And he's devoted to Russia."

"So why's he been selling them out?" asked Otto.

"You didn't listen," said Smith. "I said he's devoted to *Russia*, not to the Soviets. He was, of course, once upon a time, like all good Russians. But the higher he moved up the chain of command, the more he saw of what really goes on behind the scenes of the 'People's Paradise.' How the top people live in luxury while the ordinary people scrape out a living. The Soviet concentration camps. About two years ago, he came to us because he said he was sick of what the Soviets had done to Russia. He feels they betrayed the Russian people and his country and have turned it into a dictator state. He's worried that what they've done to his own country they'll do the to the rest of the world, if they get the chance. That's why he's been helping us."

"And what's the problem?"

"It looks as if his cover's been blown," said Smith. "We've got bugs in different government buildings in Moscow, and, from transcripts of some recent phone calls, it looks like their top brass are getting suspicious of Varentsov. If they grab him, they'll torture him and get everything he knows about us from him. Names, contact places. Everything. We've got hundreds of our agents out there who are at risk if they get to work on him."

"Is Varentsov aware the game's up?"

"Not as far as we know," said Smith. "At the moment the Soviets are just going about their normal business, not arousing suspicion. But when they move, they'll move fast. Which is why we have to try and move first and get him out."

"Out from Moscow?"

"From East Berlin. Berlin is one of the colonel's areas of operation, and he's due to go there for a meeting with his opposite number in the Stasi in two days' time. Which is why you've got the job. You look German, you speak fluent German . . ."

"I *am* German," put in Otto with a smile.

"Just make sure you remember that while you're in East Berlin," said Smith.

Smith passed a photo over to Otto. The man in the photo was in his late fifties, a stern expression on his face as he looked at the photographer. On the chest of his military tunic were rows of medals. Colonel Varentsov.

"So you'll recognize him," said Smith.

"How will he know me?" asked Otto.

"He won't," replied Smith. "We've got a password set up in case anything should go wrong and we had to get him out in a hurry. The password is 'oddjob,' and in English, not in German or Russian."

Otto frowned.

"Oddjob?"

"It's the name of a character in some spy books this limey guy writes. James Bond books."

"Oh yeah," Otto nodded. "I've never read them."

"Get that word to Varentsov and he'll know to trust you." Smith took the photo back from Otto. "One thing, if you're caught by the Soviets, we don't know you. You'll be just an American businessman up to some weird thing behind the Iron Curtain because it's where his family came from or something, nothing to do with us."

"Clear," nodded Otto. "So, when do I leave?"

"As soon as you pack your bag," said Smith. "Collect your passport and tickets and the schedule of operations from my secretary on your way out."

Now, in Berlin, Otto walked down the street, looking at all the new buildings that towered over the busy streets. He took in the parks where people sat on benches and fed pigeons or played games of chess. It was hard to think that less than twenty years ago most of this city had been rubble. Now it was a city of ultramodern buildings of concrete and glass, with the older buildings that had remained standing during the Allied bombing dwarfed by the new architecture.

He guessed he was being followed, as Smith had said. That didn't matter. He was heading for the American embassy, as any normal American businessman would, to get his papers in order and advise the embassy staff what he intended to be up to during his stay.

"Checking Berlin for a possible new plastics factory," that was his cover story.

Inside the reception area of the embassy he went through the procedures with the desk clerks and then into the embassy itself. He went up to the second floor where, as he came out of the elevator, he was met by someone he recognized from his early training at Langley, Chuck Mitford.

"Mr. Klaus," said Chuck. "I'm Charles Mitford. I understand you're here to talk about plastics."

Otto shook Chuck's hand.

"Not just plastics, *extruded* plastics," he replied.

"Then let's hope we can help you," said Chuck. "What exactly are you looking for?"

"Good-quality labor and about three acres of space," said Otto.

Chuck smiled again.

"Then you've come to the right place," he said. "Please follow me and we'll show you what we've got."

As they both stepped back into the elevator, Otto reflected that, even though they had recognized each other, ground rules said that they still had to go through the password routine.

Neither Otto nor Chuck spoke as the elevator went down. It gave Otto more time to think about the "schedule of operations," as Smith had called it. The Plan.

Soon after the Berlin Wall had been built, a tunnel had been constructed from the subbasement of the Embassy toward the East. Officially the tunnel didn't exist. Very few people even knew of its existence.

The other end of the tunnel came out in the cellar of a derelict building in the Eastern Sector. So far the tunnel hadn't been used for any operations. It had been decided to keep it in reserve until something major required its use. That time was now.

The elevator stopped at the subbasement level, and Chuck got out, Otto following. Otto followed Chuck along the corridor, and then through a series of doors.

SPIES AND SPECIAL FORCES

At each door, Chuck keyed in a security code on a panel to unlock the door. During their journey, Chuck chattered cheerfully about the great prospects for the plastics industry in Berlin, and Otto responded with equal enthusiasm.

Finally they came to a door where Chuck not only keyed in a security code on the display panel but also pressed his hand flat against a metal plate. The heavy door opened slowly, and Chuck and Otto stepped through into a long corridor. They were in the tunnel to the East.

The door closed slowly behind them.

"Fingerprint verification," explained Chuck. "The ultimate in security. We can talk in safety from here."

"Clothes?" inquired Otto.

"Everything's here waiting for you," said Chuck. He indicated a suitcase on the ground at the entrance to the tunnel. "Clothes for you for the East. Briefcase with your cover stuff. Plus overalls for Varentsov, if you get him."

"I'll get him," said Otto grimly. "There's too much at stake if I don't."

Chuck indicated a small grille set into the wall.

"When you get back, just speak into this. Someone will be listening out for you the whole time."

"Thanks," said Otto.

He was already taking the clothes out from the suitcase and changing into them. The jacket and trousers were shabby, much-mended in parts. The shirt was creased and stained. The shoes were old and worn.

"Only the top brass wear good clothes in the East," explained Chuck. "You don't want to stand out." He shot Otto a quizzical look. "Anything else you need?"

The Cold War: "Escape from the East"

"No," replied Otto. "Just some luck."

"Then here's wishing you that," said Chuck. "Good luck."

They shook hands again, then Chuck went back through the security door. Otto walked the one and a half miles along the dimly lit tunnel. In his hand he carried the shabby briefcase, which contained some well-worn school books and the overalls for Varentsov. When he reached the other end of the tunnel, he climbed the metal ladder that took him up to a metal trapdoor. He lifted it carefully and looked out. It came out into the low subcellar. There was a smell of earth and rotting wood.

He climbed out, dropped the metal trapdoor shut behind him, and kicked some of the earth loosely over it to hide it. Then he went to the wooden trapdoor in the low wooden ceiling and pushed that up.

This brought him out into a cellar proper. It was littered with debris of all sorts among piles of rubble. The place stank.

Otto found the rickety wooden stairs that led up to the ground floor. Here the wood gave way to cement, but the cement was cracked and had broken away in places, with pieces of rusting metal showing through.

Otto walked through the derelict ground floor of the building and then out into a yard. As with the building, the yard bore all the signs of dereliction and ruin. It was just a few steps to cross the yard to the unlocked wooden door, and then Otto was out in the street. He was in East Berlin.

Gray, Otto decided. That was what he felt East Berlin was like. The buildings were gray, the faces of the people were gray. There were very few smiles.

SPIES AND SPECIAL FORCES

As he approached the huge building at the corner of Normannenstrasse and Friedrichstrasse that housed the Stasi HQ, he couldn't help but feel a bolt of fear rising up from his stomach. How many thousands of people had been taken in through those doors and never come out again. Or come out wrecks of their former selves after torture and beatings. And he was going in voluntarily.

From information Langley had received from former prisoners of the Stasi, Otto knew which door housed the main reception for the public, and he headed for it now. On his way he was stopped four times by different armed guards who patrolled outside the building. Each one asked him his business, checked the contents of his briefcase, and then passed him on to another. Finally he was allowed into the reception area itself.

Perhaps it was his imagination, but to Otto the whole interior smelled of horror and fear. It was a place that was hard to get into but even harder to get out of. But this was the only way he had a hope of getting to Varentsov.

Otto went to the reception officer, a hard-faced man in uniform who glared at him from behind a battered desk.

"Yes?" the officer demanded.

Otto shuffled his feet and gave shifty glances to either side of him, as befitted a potential informer, before saying, "My name is Otto Klaus. I am a teacher. I wish to report possible treason by some of the parents of the children I teach."

The officer's expression didn't change.

"Papers," he snapped and held out his hand.

Otto reached into his jacket pocket and then handed

over the East German identification papers Chuck had supplied in the suitcase. The officer scanned them, again without expression, and then handed them back to Otto.

"Take a seat over there," he ordered Otto, indicating a row of hard wooden chairs.

Otto nodded meekly, went to the chairs and sat down.

Otto had chosen this excuse as a way of getting into Stasi headquarters because he knew that it was illegal for East Berliners to watch Western TV programs or listen to Western radio. Teachers in East Germany were urged to find out from their pupils what programs their parents watched or listened to at home, and, if the programs were from the West, to report their parents to the authorities. The parents would be charged with treason. Otto was a teacher coming in with that information, not urgent enough for him to be seen quickly, but important enough for him to be allowed to stay and wait at Stasi HQ.

Otto counted on the slowness of the Communist bureaucratic process, where processing even the simplest form could take hours and sometimes days, to allow him to stay and keep watch.

The minutes ticked by and became an hour. Very few people came in. Once the outer doors burst open and two armed men came in dragging a man. They disappeared through some doors, and then that was it for another thirty minutes. Otto sat and waited. As the second hour dragged by Otto began to worry that he'd got it wrong. Maybe Varentsov had already been arrested. Maybe even now the colonel was on his way back to Moscow. Just as he was thinking this, the main doors opened and two armed Stasi men marched in. Behind them came a tall, thickset man. He was dressed in civilian clothes and a heavy overcoat, but there was no mistaking the cropped gray hair, the set features of that face. It was Colonel Varentsov.

As Varentsov strode across the floor of the reception area, two armed Stasi men in front, two behind, Otto called out, "Oddjob!"

The effect was startling. The two Stasi men in front of Varentsov turned on Otto, their automatic weapons leveled at him, their fingers poised to fire, and Otto's throat went dry. They're going to kill me! he realized.

"Stop!" came the snapped command from Varentsov. Turning to the two Stasi men behind him, the Colonel pointed his finger at Otto and barked, "Bring that man to me!"

The next moment Otto found himself unceremoniously dragged out of his chair and hustled toward Varentsov.

"My apologies!" begged Otto. "I meant no disrespect! I thought you were someone I knew, a neighbor of mine, Karl Oddjob."

Varentsov frowned thoughtfully. Then he snapped to his armed Stasi guards, "Take him out to my car and put him in the back."

Otto found himself gripped firmly and marched at speed out of the reception area. Outside the two Stasi men hurried Otto toward a large black car with darkened windows. One of the guards opened the rear door of the car, and then Otto was bundled in. The driver of the car looked briefly back at Otto in the rearview mirror, then turned his eyes to the front again. As a driver for the KGB, he knew it was better to see nothing.

The Cold War: "Escape from the East"

Otto heard Varentsov snap, "I will deal with this!"

Then the colonel climbed into the back of the car beside Otto and slammed the door shut.

"Alexanderplatz," he commanded the driver.

The car moved off.

Varentsov sat in silence, his face showing no emotion as they drove. They drove for about five minutes, and then Varentsov barked at the driver: "Stop here!"

The driver pulled into the curb. Varentsov leaned forward toward the driver, as if to whisper something to him. Otto saw something in the colonel's fist as he tapped the driver on the side of the neck. The driver jerked round, startled, putting his hand to his neck. Then the driver's eyes rolled upward and he fell forward.

"He is merely unconscious," said Varentsov. "He will be out for thirty minutes. Is that enough time?"

"I hope so," said Otto. From his briefcase he took the pair of overalls. "Put these on. I hope they fit."

"They will," said Varentsov as he struggled out of his overcoat and jacket in the back of the car and then pulled on the overalls.

A few minutes later both men were heading toward Reinhardtstrasse. Otto led the way, running through the memorized map of the area in his head. They were two miles from the derelict building that housed the tunnel back to the West.

"Do not walk too fast," muttered Varentsov to Otto. "Ordinary workers do not hurry. There is nowhere good to hurry to these days."

Otto forced himself to slow down. So far so good, but in less than thirty minutes Varentsov's driver would wake and the alarm would be raised. Sooner, if someone discovered Varentsov's car abandoned. That meant they couldn't afford to dawdle.

They had been walking for about fifteen minutes in silence when they heard the sound of police sirens, and Otto stopped and looked around.

"It could be for anything and anyone," said Varentsov. "Arrests are commonplace."

"But if they are after you, they'll be checking all the streets near the Wall," said Otto. "We've got to speed up."

Now Otto could hear the sound of sirens getting nearer.

"How do you plan to get us through the Wall?" asked Varentsov.

"I'll tell you that when we get there," said Otto.

"You do not trust me?" asked Varentsov.

"I don't trust the fact that we may get caught before we get there. If that happens, with luck they'll shoot me and the secret will die with me. What you don't know, you can't tell."

The colonel nodded.

"Very good," he said. "I approve."

They were walking faster now, and for the first time Otto noticed that Varentsov was limping.

"You are hurt?" he said.

Varentsov laughed.

"I was hurt many times. Three times in the right leg. 1942, 1943, and 1944. The Germans must have had it in for my poor leg."

Otto could feel his chest starting to hurt. It wasn't just the speed at which they were walking while trying not to look as if they were going fast, it was the fear. The sirens were definitely getting louder.

He could see the corner of Reinhardtstrasse now. Not far to go.

And then he heard the sound of a car coming up fast behind them. There was a blur as it raced past, then a squeal of brakes as it screeched to a halt in front of them.

The doors of the car flew open and two policemen leaped out of the car, pulling their guns from their holsters.

"Hande hoch!" called one. "Put your hands up!"

"What have we done . . . ?" Otto began to protest plaintively, acting the part of the innocent bystander.

The nearest policeman leveled his gun menacingly at Otto.

"Hands up or I shoot!"

Otto hesitated. He daren't let himself be taken prisoner. It would be as he had told Varentsov — he would have to die rather than let the Stasi interrogators take him apart and get any information from him. Otto took a deep breath and stepped toward the policeman with the gun, half closing his eyes as he did so against the bullet.

BANG! BANG!

Otto opened his eyes, bewildered. There was no pain.

Then he saw the two policemen. One lay on the pavement, the other lay sprawled near the police car. Both were dead.

Otto turned toward the colonel as he slipped his pistol back into the pocket of his overalls.

"You?!" he said, awed.

"I was pistol champion of my tank destroyer regiment," said Varentsov. "I still practice every day. This has been today's practice. Now, I suggest we move."

Otto nodded. He still felt odd. He should have been dead, but instead he was alive and running toward the wooden door that led into the yard of the derelict building, with Varentsov following close behind him. Through the door, across the yard, stumbling over piles of debris and rubble as they ran, then they were into the ruined building and heading down to the cellar.

Forty minutes later, Otto was relaxing with Chuck Mitford in his office inside the American embassy, safe back in West Berlin. At the same time, Varentsov was in a suite of offices at the top of the embassy being debriefed by senior CIA and Pentagon officials.

"Good operation, Otto," said Chuck, sipping his coffee.

"So far," commented Otto. "We've still got to get Varentsov out of Berlin. The Soviets will know he's here in the embassy."

"Relax," said Chuck. "That's a job for the diplomats. So long as he's here, he's safe. This is American territory." Then Chuck gave a rueful sigh. "Pity about the tunnel, though. Because one thing's for sure, the Commies'll be pulling apart every building in the area where those two cops died. Guess we'll have to close the tunnel permanently before they find it. Still, we lost one, we won a big one." And Chuck raised his coffee cup toward Otto in salute.

"Cheers!" he said. "Gesundheit!"

What happened next:

During the late 1980s, as the Soviet Union started to crumble, tensions between the East and the Western bloc nations eased. 1989 saw first the opening, and then the collapse, of the Berlin Wall, and the end of the Soviet Union.

However, for the CIA, as one threat receded, others arose, in the form of terrorism. The war goes on.

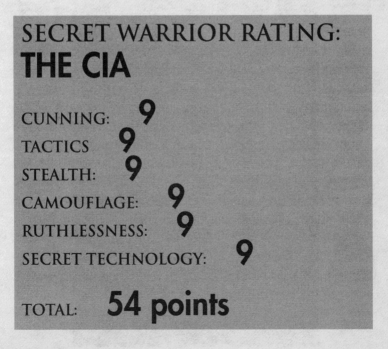

SECRET WARRIOR RATING:
THE CIA

CUNNING: 9

TACTICS 9

STEALTH: 9

CAMOUFLAGE: 9

RUTHLESSNESS: 9

SECRET TECHNOLOGY: 9

TOTAL: 54 points

6 2099: "Morphers"

As we continue on into the 21st century we are seeing incredible developments in the biosciences. From the early days of matching tissues for organ transplants, we are now seeing organs being grown for spare part surgery, human cloning, and genetic modifications that appear to be more a part of science fiction than science fact. But science fiction and science fact have always been two sides of the same coin, with some science fiction writers developing an idea from science fact, and some scientists inspired to turn a science fiction concept into reality. This story is a fictional look at the spies of the future.

THE HARDWARE

The hardware is us: the human body is the raw material for biotechnologists' modifications and adaptations that eventually produced Morphers.

2099: "MORPHERS"

The history behind the story

In the late twentieth century, certain dictators created doubles via cosmetic surgery as a precaution against assassination. In the 21st century, the next step was the creation of doubles by cloning using DNA. The next step was the development of genetically created "Morphers": humans who could take on the identity of another person just by absorbing DNA through the skin of their fingertips. Once the technology had been developed, Morphers were used as more than just doubles; they were used as spies who could infiltrate anywhere, taking on a whole new persona at a touch, but still retaining their true identity. With Morphers virtually impossible to spot, even with retinal scans and voiceprints, whoever used a Morpher had access to the most powerful secret weapon . . . *ever!*

General Carlos Barranquilla sat on the porch of his hideaway headquarters deep in the Colombian jungle and looked out at his men, his soldiers, all heavily armed, as they moved about inside the heavily fortified compound. Elsewhere, hidden throughout the jungle, were more of his men, guarding every road or river that came to this small hidden township. A feeling of satisfaction filled the general as he took all this in. He insisted on being addressed by his rank, even by his most trusted and oldest friends, because it helped to maintain discipline. Because what was an army unless it had strong discipline?

To some in the outside world he was a gangster, a terrorist, a drug racketeer, a jungle warlord. But here he was a king, an emperor, ruler of an army of 20,000 fighters and their families. Here, in this stronghold, he was untouchable. And very soon he would have his revenge on those who tried to hunt him down and destroy him. The president of the United States, for one.

"The Yankee is here, General!"

The general turned and saw his trusted second-in-command, Colonel Raul Monteria, standing to attention just beside him. Of course he had heard the helicopter coming in to land at the strip outside the compound five minutes ago. The Yankee. Brett Thompson. The dealer, the middleman said by some to be the most crooked man on the planet. The man who could fix anything. In the past two years Thompson had fixed many things for the general: the assassinations of politicians in the United States who kept calling for his extradition, the wholesale robberies of banks across the world, the export of thousands of tons of drugs in bulk into Europe and North America. And all without being caught. Perhaps some mules had been arrested, some terrorists killed, but the Yankee always stayed one step ahead. Yes, Thompson really could fix anything.

"Good morning, General!" came the voice of Thompson. The tall American saluted smartly and then mounted the steps to join the general on the porch.

"How was your journey?" asked the general.

"The usual," replied Thompson. "Expensive. It seems every government in the world has put a price on my head, so moving about costs more all the time. So, I hear you have a job for me?"

The general smiled.

"I like a man who does not mess around with small talk but gets straight to the point," he said.

Thompson smiled and shrugged.

"For a man like me, time is money," he said. "I start talking about the weather, I'm wasting thousands of dollars. So, what do you need?"

"I need a Morpher," said the general.

The smile vanished from Thompson's face.

"Are you serious?" he asked.

"Deadly serious," nodded the general.

A look of concern crossed the American's face.

"If we're going to talk about this, we shouldn't do it here, out in the open," he said. "My government has spies everywhere."

"Not here," said the general confidently. "All my men are loyal."

"I wasn't thinking of your men," said Thompson. "I was thinking of things like a satellite video filming us even as we sit here, with a lip-reader sitting at a TV screen up in Langley and telling the CIA chiefs every word we're saying."

The general thought about this for a moment, then he nodded.

"Very well," he said. Turning to Raul standing beside them, he said, "Come, Colonel, we will go inside and talk with Mr. Thompson."

"Whoa!" said Thompson, holding up his hand. "If we're going to be talking about Morphers, then this is just you and me. No one else."

The general scowled, angry.

"Colonel Monteria is my oldest and most trusted comrade. I would trust him with my life."

"That may be," said Thompson. "But six months ago my oldest and most trusted colleague, my own kid brother, tried to kill me for a reward of ten million dollars. You trust who you like, General, I trust no one. That's why I'm still alive. And I don't have a jungle kingdom to hide in and keep me safe, I'm out there in the big wide world." Thompson shook his head. "Sorry, General, but it's my life on the line, and on this topic it's you and me one to one, in private, or not at all."

The general thought it over. What Thompson said

made sense, but the general also trusted very few people. And although Thompson had shown himself to be true in their many encounters and dealings these past years, the general did not trust him. However, for his plan to succeed, he needed to get hold of a Morpher, and if anyone could fix that, that man was Brett Thompson.

"Very well," he nodded at last. To Monteria he said, "Colonel, we will be going into my private room. You will stay on guard to make sure that no one else comes in. When we have finished, I will come out first. If Mr. Thompson should come out of the room without me, shoot him at once."

The general turned to Thompson and said, "I hope you don't take my orders personally."

"Not at all," shrugged Thompson. "I'd do the same if I were in your shoes. Like I say, trust no one."

Thompson followed the general into the small room off the porch. The door shut behind them.

The general motioned Thompson to one of the two chairs in the room and then sat down himself.

"Now," said the general. "If what I have heard is true, these creatures called Morphers could be a very powerful weapon."

"The most powerful," nodded Thompson in agreement. "But they cost. We are talking big, big money."

"The money is no object," said the general. "The return on this investment will be enormous. Am I right in thinking that these creatures can take on the shape of any person?"

Again Thompson nodded. "It was the next development after human cloning," he said. "A human clone that could be imprinted, like a blank recording medium just waiting for an image to be put on it. It's all done by DNA. They absorb the DNA of the person they're chosen to copy just by touch, and that DNA writes a new program for the Morpher: the face changes, the body shape, the hair color, the voice, everything. Even right down to memories." Thompson chuckled. "That's what makes them so perfect," he continued. "You put someone through plastic surgery to make them look like someone else, the whole thing's blown as soon as they start talking. The accent's not quite right. They certainly wouldn't remember things from childhood, or even people they'd met a while ago. With a Morpher, everything's automatic."

"Excellent!" smiled the general. "And you can get one?"

"I can get *everything*," said Thompson confidently. "You should know that. So, what do you want this Morpher for?"

"To become president of the U.S.A.," replied the general.

Thompson looked at the general in surprise and then chuckled appreciatively.

"Wow!" he commented. "I can see why you say 'money no object.' If it's your Morpher in the White House, you control foreign policy. So, no more money spent on chasing General Barranquilla and his army."

"Even better than that!" said the general enthusiastically. "We can expand and be supported every inch of the way by our very own president!"

"One problem with all this," put in Thompson thoughtfully. "America is a democracy. We hold elections. If the great American public doesn't like what your boy is doing, they'll kick him out and there'll be a new president in the White House. What happens then?"

The general chuckled, almost swelling with supreme confidence.

"Why, if that happens, then our Morpher congratulates him with a handshake . . ."

Thompson's face lit up in delighted and impressed understanding.

"And once more your boy becomes the new president!" he said. "And so it goes on forever! It's great!"

"Of course it is," nodded the general. "All I need is to get hold of a Morpher. Can you do that?"

Thompson nodded.

"Like I said, I can get hold of anything. Consider it done."

He and the general stood up, Thompson holding out his hand for the traditional handshake to close the deal. The general took the American's hand and clasped it firmly. As he did so a strange feeling began to take him over. It was as if he couldn't move. He tried to remove his hand from the American's grasp, but it seemed frozen solid. He opened his mouth to speak, but no words came out.

As he looked at Thompson, the face of the American seemed to be changing, a mustache growing swiftly on his upper lip, his eyebrows becoming thicker, heavier. Thompson was talking and the general strained to hear.

"There are a couple of things you ought to know," said Thompson. "For one thing, Thompson got caught by the CIA a week ago. For another, we new Morphers have a swift-acting poison in our sweat glands that we use to immobilize our victims. It paralyzes at a touch when we switch it on. You might be interested to know that it's been developed from the venom of a snake from down here in South America."

The general's head was swimming now. All his limbs were without feeling. His heart was slowing down. He could barely hear, barely see . . . but he saw enough before his eyes dimmed completely to see that the face of the man in front of him was now his own. He was looking at himself, General Carlos Barranquilla.

"One other thing," said his own face in his own voice. "We've also been developed with one extra amazing function. As well as absorbing the DNA of our victims and becoming them, at the same time we transmit the DNA of the last person we morphed into the victim, so the new victim becomes the old. It's a complete transference. Wonderful, isn't it!"

But the general was past hearing anything.

The Morpher, now in the form of General Carlos Barranquilla, carefully lowered the dead body that now looked like Thompson to the floor. A swift change of clothes, from Thompson's dark suit to the general's jungle fatigues, and the conversion was complete.

The new general took out his pistol, aimed it at the dead body, and pulled the trigger.

Immediately the door burst open and Colonel Monteria crashed into the room, his automatic rifle at the ready.

The general held up his hand to stop him.

"No problem, Colonel," he said. "The American tried to kill me. I killed him first."

With that the general strode out of the room and onto

the porch. He looked up at the sky. About now a satellite would be going over, recording everything that was going on. He took off his jungle hat and fanned himself with it, then put it back on his head. It was the signal to his masters back in Langley that the operation had been successful. Tomorrow, General Barranquilla would be ordering his troops out into the jungle and straight into the traps that would be waiting for them.

The Day of the Morpher had arrived.

What Happened Next:

With the ever-accelerating pace of new discoveries in biosciences, anything can happen!

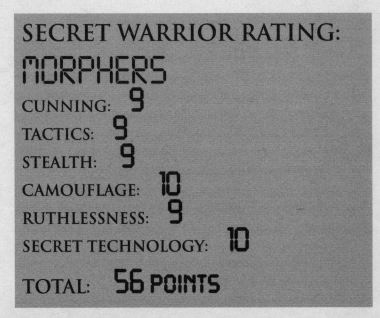

SECRET WARRIOR RATING:

MORPHERS

CUNNING: 9

TACTICS: 9

STEALTH: 9

CAMOUFLAGE: 10

RUTHLESSNESS: 9

SECRET TECHNOLOGY: 10

TOTAL: 56 POINTS

ABOUT THE AUTHOR

Jim Eldridge has spent most of his life undercover. He has been caught up in combat action since his birth in a war zone during a bombing raid in 1944. A man of a thousand faces and with many aliases in his past, he relaxes with pursuits such as mountain climbing, desert trekking, swimming with sharks, and meditation.